The Data Gaze

SOCIETY AND SPACE SERIES

The *Society and Space* series explores the fascinating relationship between the spatial and the social. Each title draws on a range of modern and historical theories to offer important insights into the key cultural and political topics of our times, including migration, globalisation, race, gender, sexuality and technology. These stimulating and provocative books combine high intellectual standards with contemporary appeal for students of politics, international relations, sociology, philosophy, and human geography.

Also in this series:

Migration, Ethics and Power
Dan Bulley

Surveillance and Space
Francisco R. Klauser

Geographies of Violence
Marcus A. Doel

Circulation and Urbanization
Ross E. Adams

The Data Gaze

Gaze

Capitalism, Power and Perception

David Beer

Los Angeles | London | New Delhi
Singapore | Washington DC | Melbourne

Los Angeles | London | New Delhi
Singapore | Washington DC | Melbourne

SAGE Publications Ltd
1 Oliver's Yard
55 City Road
London EC1Y 1SP

SAGE Publications Inc.
2455 Teller Road
Thousand Oaks, California 91320

SAGE Publications India Pvt Ltd
B 1/I 1 Mohan Cooperative Industrial Area
Mathura Road
New Delhi 110 044

SAGE Publications Asia-Pacific Pte Ltd
3 Church Street
#10-04 Samsung Hub
Singapore 049483

© David Beer 2019

First published 2019

Editor: Robert Rojek
Assistant editor: John Nightingale
Production editor: Katherine Haw
Copyeditor: Jane Fricker
Proofreader: Lynda Watson
Indexer: Elizabeth Ball
Marketing manager: Susheel Gokarakonda
Cover design: Wendy Scott
Typeset by: C&M Digitals (P) Ltd, Chennai, India
Printed in the UK

Library of Congress Control Number: 2018944629

British Library Cataloguing in Publication data

A catalogue record for this book is available from
the British Library

ISBN 978-1-5264-3691-7
ISBN 978-1-5264-3692-4 (pbk)

At SAGE we take sustainability seriously. Most of our products are printed in the UK using responsibly sourced
papers and boards. When we print overseas we ensure sustainable papers are used as measured by the
PREPS grading system. We undertake an annual audit to monitor our sustainability.

In memory of Bill, Louie, Enid and Derick.

Contents

About the Author

David Beer is Reader in Sociology at the University of York. He is the author of *Metric Power, Punk Sociology, Popular Culture and New Media: The Politics of Circulation*, and *New Media: The Key Concepts* (with Nicholas Gane), and the editor of *The Social Power of Algorithms*.

Acknowledgements

First, I would like to thank Daryl Martin. This book emerged after something he said to me following a presentation I gave on the material that later became Chapter 3 of this book. Daryl's typically thoughtful intervention gave me the germ of an idea that developed in the months that followed. I would like to thank Stuart Elden as the *Society and Space* book series editor: his enthusiasm and guidance were very much appreciated. Similar thanks go to Robert Rojek at SAGE: his interest in my work helped a great deal with energising and focusing this project. Rosie Smith also made an invaluable contribution. I was granted a small amount of funding from the Department of Sociology at the University of York; with this funding I recruited Rosie to gather the various documents used in Chapter 4. Rosie's careful and thorough approach meant that I had a wealth of materials to work with. Beyond this I would like to thank my colleagues for discussing ideas. Particular thanks go to Katy Sian, Ruth Penfold-Mounce, Wes Lin, Joanna Latimer, Gareth Millington, Rolland Munro, John Gardner, Nisha Kapoor, Andrew Webster and Nathan Manning, who were all good enough to discuss some of the specific ideas I was working on for this book. My gratitude also goes to the reviewers of the book manuscript. Taking the time to read and provide such useful comments on the book is an act of collaboration and support in a pressured environment, I am exceptionally grateful to them for their help.

Chapters 2 and 3 substantially rework and extend two published journal articles. Chapter 2 extends the ideas in the article 'Envisioning the power of data analytics' which was published in *Information, Communication & Society* (Vol. 21, issue 3). Chapter 3 is based around the article 'The data analytics industry and the promises of real-time knowing' which was published in the *Journal of Cultural Economy* (Vol. 10, issue 1). Thanks go to the editors and reviewers of those journals for their help with shaping the ideas covered in those two chapters and to Taylor & Francis for permission to use these articles. Finally, as always, special thanks are reserved for Erik and Martha. Understandably, they never read past the acknowledgements page – Erik and Martha you can stop reading now, I hope everyone else will carry on.

1

Introducing the Data Gaze

Standing at the centre of Jacques Derrida's (1996) famous lecture on the archive is the shadowy figure of the 'archon'. Displaying a strong sense of duty, ennobled by authority and carrying a whiff of the sinister, these archons not only controlled what was to be included within the walls of the archive they also dictated the means by which these documents were classified and rendered retrievable. Consequently, through their management of the ordering of these official spaces of accumulation, they had control over what that archive could be used to say. For Derrida, the power of the archive rested in the hands of these archons and was embodied in their practices, judgements and selections. Derrida's point is that when data and metadata accumulate, it is those who oversee its storage and retrieval that have the real sway.

If we fast forward to the present, we might wonder who is saying what with the many and varied types of archived data that are now so central to the functioning of the social world. Ranging from the hyperbolic to the cynical, there are many competing and polarised perspectives on the role and social significance of data. We can cut through some of the fog by asking one direct question: with all these amassing data about people, places, organisations and nation states, who has the power to speak with those data? Or, perhaps more fittingly, who has the power to speak with *our* data? Crucial to answering such a question is an understanding of the new types of knowledge that are emerging along with an understanding of how that knowledge achieves authority, credibility and legitimacy. This question may seem straightforward but it is tough to answer. This book thinks about how we might begin to formulate some answers. The underpinning principle of the book is that we need to gain a greater understanding of the industry that has emerged around these new data and we need to explore how data-led processes spread, how data-informed knowledge is legitimated and how this industry approaches and frames data. In short, we need to examine these new forms of knowledge and emergent industry in order to appreciate the expansion of an inescapable gaze and its unending scrutiny. Understanding the changing nature of knowledge is a prerequisite for resisting, challenging and questioning the interventions and consequences that this *data gaze* affords.

In a detailed and compelling account of the emergence of what has been referred to as the 'data revolution', Rob Kitchin (2014) outlines exactly how new forms of data have come to reshape and implicate the social world in all sorts of ways. Kitchin (2014: 2–4) also helpfully describes what these data are, how they can be defined and what it is that they have changed. He notes, by way of a starting point, that data are 'commonly understood to be the raw materials produced by abstracting the world into categories, measures and other representational forms – numbers, characters, symbols, images, sounds, electro-magnetic waves, bits – that constitute the building blocks from which information and knowledge are created' (Kitchin, 2014: 1). Kitchin proceeds by elaborating on this broader definition by adding detail and explicating different types of data. Of course, with a word that is being so widely appropriated, which is certainly the case for 'data', there are likely to be some issues with the definition. Data is a term that already has a long history of quite diverse use (Rosenberg, 2013), and this problem has escalated with all the talk of data and big data in recent years (as captured by Kitchin, 2014). However, rather than adding to or selecting only one of these definitions, this book will focus instead on the appropriation of the term and the various ways it is deployed. A fixed definition would hinder the explorations I provide, largely because I want to see how data are defined and made up by this industry. The way data is spoken of and defined reveals something of its materiality and the agendas that are at play. It is important, I would suggest, to see how data are spoken of, invented and put to work. We need to see how data are made up conceptually as a part of the advancement of data-led thinking and in response to these changing infrastructures, practices and forms of knowledge (Beer, 2016a).

Despite the agenda-setting work of writers like Kitchin and many of the others that I will draw upon in this book, there remains something to be said about those organisations, software packages and individuals who are working to mediate data and facilitate their integration into how we live. Understanding our data-rich environment requires an understanding of the visions, infrastructures and practices that facilitate what is said with our data. We need to understand how those data are deployed and what is enunciated with and through them. We need to understand how data-rich processes spread, how they take root, what systems unfold and how they demarcate new practices and forms of knowledge. In response, this book reflects on the visions, infrastructures and practices of what have been referred to as 'data intermediaries' (Schrock and Shaffer, 2017). Centrally it asks how we can understand the data analytics industry and its growing power. To do this, and to explore how data are seen and spoken of, it develops the central concept of *the data gaze*.

It is now over a decade since Nigel Thrift (2005) wrote of the developments that he labelled 'knowing capitalism'. In that book Thrift (2005: 12) suggested that he was observing the beginning of something. Much has changed in that time, not least the presence of mobile devices, social media, embedded sensors, tracking and global positioning technologies, smartphones, on-demand consumption and the many other developments that bring new possibilities for capturing and using data. Thrift's book was published around two years before the launch of the iPhone and the rise of social media. We could conclude simply that capitalism has become more knowing in the interim – the enhancement of data collation means that organisations can know us in much greater depth than in the period when Thrift was writing his book. Perhaps this is the case; I think though that there is more to be said than this cursory observation might at first suggest.

More recently attempts at understanding the role of data within capitalism have turned to the notion of the 'platform'. At around the same time that Nick Srnicek (2017) was working on his book *Platform Capitalism*, Paul Langley and Andrew Leyshon (2017) were collaborating on a detailed journal article with the same title. Both take data as being central to capitalism and note the importance of understanding the different platforms that facilitate the extraction and circulation of data. Srnicek (2017: 6) argues that:

> … capitalism has turned to data as one way to maintain economic growth and vitality in the face of a sluggish production sector. In the twenty-first century, on the basis of changes in digital technologies, data have become increasingly central to firms and their relations with workers, customers, and other capitalists. The platform has emerged as a new business model, capable of extracting and controlling immense amounts of data.

The platform, in this vision, acts as the foundation upon which data are utilised. These platforms manage the circulation of data (Langley and Leyshon, 2017: 25), with business models built around these features for lending, exchange, service provision, and so on. This is a form of capitalism in which, Srnicek (2017: 41) claims, 'data increasingly became a central resource'. Langley and Leyshon (2017: 19) use the concept of 'platform capitalism' to foreground the connection of the 'infrastructural and intermediary qualities of the platform'. Platforms, in this account, intermediate the flows of data.

The aim in this introductory chapter is not to explore all of the possible ways that we can conceptualise the relations between capitalism and data, yet concepts such as 'platform capitalism' illustrate just how central data have become to the functioning of contemporary capitalism and capitalist society. As I will illustrate, notions of value are often woven into the uses and understandings of data as well as the visions and promises that are attached to them. This makes data a routine and structurally significant part of the ordering of the social world, and it suggests that it might stretch far into our lives – perhaps beyond even the reach of capitalism. Focusing upon the role of analytics, as I do in this book, inevitably reveals something of these platforms and the use of data within such advancing modes of capitalism.

Of course, all of this is not to say that we need a totalising vision of a homogeneous capitalism in which the role and spread of data are the same everywhere. We know that this would be a mistake, as is made clear, for instance, in Kalyan Sanyal's (2007: 45) accounts of 'post-colonial capitalism'. The relations between data and capitalism are inevitably uneven and reveal underpinning regional and national variations, variegated political economies and geographical inequalities. I start instead from the perspective that, as with capitalism more generally (Peck and Theodore, 2007), the use of data is likely to have uneven geographies and be variegated in its deployment. I have discussed the role of data and metrics in the political economy in much more detail in my previous book, *Metric Power*; here I wish to deal much more directly with the implied question of the intermediary and the industry that facilitates the circulation of data. One way to avoid the problems associated with a more general understanding of data is to begin to unpick the systems through which those data circulate.

However we might conceptualise the relations between data and capitalism, the accumulation and analysis of data does not happen by accident. We are not simply gliding on rails through predetermined forms of an advancing capitalism. There is work being done to make this happen. A key thing to remember, I would suggest, is that the claims being made about the possibilities and potentials of data represent a kind of boundary work. As I will discuss in Chapters 2 and 3, these claims are concerned with crossing thresholds and pushing back frontiers. These claims are wrapped up with *a veneer of knowing* that aims to draw people into a data rationality. The promises of making us better people, healthier, more efficient, better at connecting, interacting and choosing are coupled with ideas about what can be done to us with data, shaping who we vote for, our performance levels, our credit worthiness, our desirability as customers, and so on. These are instances of this boundary work aimed at intensifying and expanding the reach of data analytics. Data-led processes are actively being spread and a space has opened up in which the data analytics industry has stepped and grown. As data amass, the pressure grows to do something with those data. As the volume of data expands, opportunities are created for those who can locate value in those data. Understanding data-intensive capitalism requires an exploration of the way that data have been embraced, the rationalities that underpin them and the intensity of their application. Thrift's focus was upon 'what happened when capitalism began to intervene in, and make a business out of, thinking the everyday' (Thrift, 2005: 1). This book is about how those interventions are made possible, how they advance, how they are created and afforded, how they are legitimised and rendered desirable. In short, it is concerned with understanding *the industry of intervention* that is now active in shaping the social world in so many different ways.

It is a well-rehearsed point that data have infiltrated many aspects of our lives, that they produce actions and then circulate back into various processes, decisions and outcomes (Beer, 2013). The depth of these data circulations, as I have discussed before, is hard to fathom. This makes it difficult to track and hard for its social implications to be identified, studied and fully explored. How can we detach ourselves from this in order to really see what is happening? Data have come to implicate nearly all aspects of social life, from the workplace and employee performance (Moore, 2018), to quantified-self movements and self-tracking (Lupton, 2016; Neff and Nafus, 2016), the tracking of health (Sharon, 2017) and emotions (Davies, 2017a), to social media profiles, targeted advertising, customer monitoring, through to financial transactions and trading, as well as the governance of nation states (Karppi and Crawford, 2016), transportation systems and utilities (Dodge and Kitchin, 2009), how borders are managed and risk is assessed (Amoore, 2011) and even to the way that political campaigns are fought (Davies, 2017b). Helen Kennedy (2016: 232), in her crucial study of data mining within organisations, has argued that in this context we need to gain an appreciation of the 'new data relations'. These new data relations, Kennedy (2016: 232) points out, are 'increasingly integral to everyday social relations'. With this rise of data, the social world is being reordered in some surprising and sometimes telling ways. Such data are, of course, never raw (Gitelman and Jackson, 2013): they still need to be interpreted, to be made sense of and to be made comprehensible. Understandably we tend to turn our focus to the outcomes of these processes, the things that data make happen. This is especially the case when the consequences pop up in very visible or emotive ways in our lives – the injustices, the mistreatments, the insensitivities of data are where we are most likely, momentarily, to feel their presence. We also notice the incongruities – the misplaced advert, the strange recommendation or the moments when we are struck by the depth of the surveillance of our everyday lives.

With this social expansion of the ordering role of data there have also come new ways of knowing. More is known about populations and individuals because of the escalating data infrastructures. Out of the shadows have emerged new types of knowledge and expertise – along with this have emerged new experts, consultants and gurus, or what Nicole Aschoff (2015) has described as the 'new prophets of capital'. We can ask what this knowledge is used for, who is using it and how. We might also ask how this knowledge is connected into power dynamics and social structures, what the agendas are that reside in these new forms of knowledge and how they are tied into the expansion of the processes themselves. In this book I veer towards questions concerning the powerful notions and conceptualisations of data that have enabled or afforded the very expansion of these data-harvesting infrastructures and which have enabled data analysis to take on such a prominent role in our lives. As such, it asks how these data are understood, framed and approached. It reflects on what these reveal about claims to knowledge and how power is reinforced and deployed through data. The way in which data are seen is crucial to the power that they afford and the possibilities that are available for the expansion of data-led thinking, judgement, ordering and governance. The way that data are seen is also central to the scale of the material infrastructures as well as the hopes, promises and possibilities that are attached to those data. Being data informed is often presented as an inevitable force to yield to (as I will discuss in Chapter 2).

Overall, data are seen to provide powerful forms of knowledge and insight into the social world. Seeing into this power and understanding its machinations requires us to think about how this knowledge is framed, how it is presented, what type of expertise it evokes and authenticates, and what notions of truth and worth are bound up in these forms of knowledge. We need to see how these data are understood as well as what they can do, because it is here that the outcomes are being pre-set, where agendas are being articulated and embedded and where claims to know-how and expertise are being made.

Of course, it is important to explore how the data see us, how we are judged by data, how we are evaluated and treated, and so on. There are those who are working on such questions and who are developing fantastic, detailed and revealing accounts of data mining and data judgements in operation (see for example Amoore, 2013; Kennedy, 2016; Moore, 2018). As I will show here, we also need to explore how the data themselves are seen, how they are looked upon, how they are regarded and how that then shapes the forms of perception that are at play once the data are utilised in various analytic outcomes. An understanding of how data are seen is required before we can fully understand how they are used to see us. That is what this book aims to do. It aims to see the implicit limits and parameters that are being set into data before or whilst they are utilised. What is the underlying mode of thinking that resides in data use? What rationalities and ways of thinking are part of how data-led processes find their way into our lives? These are the types of questions that I hope to answer here. This is a book that is about the formation and spread of data-informed knowledge. It is about the *notions of value* and *ideals of living* that are coded into the very agendas and social programmes within which data are involved. It is about the formation of analytical spaces and technologies that structure how data are used and what can be said with them. When we think about how data are used in the social world, to order and govern, this book suggests that we should also think about the way that those data are imagined, the possibilities that they have been ascribed, to whom they lend the power to speak and what they allow to be said. This is about how authenticity and accuracy are ascribed and engraved into the materiality of the data. It is here, in this focus, that we can reveal much about what is going on, about how data-led processes spread and intensify, about how the analytics themselves play to certain composed tunes and arrangements, about how knowledge forms from certain circumscribed foundations. In other words, we cannot just concern ourselves with the outcomes of data and their analytics, much as these are powerful and important, we need to understand those outcomes by exploring how data are seen in the first place. That is to say that we need to understand the emergence of the *data gaze* in order to fully understand the consequences of how that gaze is then exercised.

As the above suggests, this book is centrally concerned with interrogating the types of knowledge, expertise and rationalities that are associated with data analytics. This is a book about the perception of data and how data become part of perception. To achieve this it takes three key steps. It begins by arguing that the way that these analytics are envisioned is central to the emergence and prominence of data at various scales of social life. It then follows these visions, in the second and third steps, out into the infrastructures and practices of data analytics. Within this, it aims to understand the powerful role of the data analytics industry and how this industry facilitates the spread and intensification of data-led processes. This book is concerned with understanding how data-led, data-driven and data-reliant forms of capitalism find their way to the inside of organisational and everyday life. This form of *data capitalism* can be thought of in very broad terms as a form of capitalism that operates through, is informed by and relies upon data. The book is concerned with the mechanisms by which such data analytic processes are integrated, incorporated and assimilated. Despite their escalating presence, there is little real sense of how these data-led ordering processes have evolved, how they work or how they have managed to seep so far into the structures in which we live. The data analytics industry that has emerged in recent years, taking advantage of the need or desire for something to be said with the rapidly accumulating data about people and populations, is now active in providing what are often referred to as *solutions* and *insights* for those who are interested in their promises of gaining *a competitive edge* or *knowing* themselves and their markets. Those data analytics are said to have a powerful analytical gaze that far exceeds the gaze of any individual (see Chapter 2). The data gaze is a concept that targets an understanding of the connections, structures and performances of power within analytics. The book will explore how the data gaze is envisioned as affording a view of futures, emotions, mobilities, interactions and structural granularity, both at a distance and close up. This data gaze, and the discourse that facilitates and informs it, is suggestive of how lives are viewed differently through data – in ever more forensic, strategic, predictive and knowing ways.

In more specific terms, this book explores the type of prosthetic vision that is said to be provided by data analytics packages of various types. This is to look at how the data are seen and also what it is that they are said to render visible – as well as what remains invisible in the 'data shadows' (Leonelli et al., 2017). The book explores the way in which the vision or gaze of data analytics is presented, imagined and deployed. The aim here is to reveal the embedded rationalising discourses that are deeply woven into data analytics. This rationalising discourse – which reflects wider norms, modes of calculative thinking, forms of governance and political ideas – is doing a significant amount of work to shape the integration and realisation of data analytics in different settings. By looking at the envisioned gaze of data analytics, we are then both tapping into wider social framings whilst also revealing the programmes of knowledge and rationalising logics that are responsible for spreading and intensifying data-led evaluations throughout the social world. Developing the concept of the *data gaze*, I suggest that this gaze, both in its material and discursive formations, is a powerful analytic, constitutive and performative social presence. The idea of using the concept of the gaze is not to privilege the visual but to show how the visual, the optic and the material are privileged in the knowledge that forms around data analytics.

To achieve this, amongst a range of other resources the book will turn to Michel Foucault's (2003) classic study *The Birth of the Clinic*.[1] Originally published in 1963 (for a discussion see Eribon, 1992: 144–5; Macey, 1995: 129), Foucault's book tells the story of the emergence of clinical-based medicine. This might seem something of a leap, with the topics seemingly quite separate, but in that book Foucault explores the changing role of the expert gaze whilst also addressing the rationalising discourse that accompanies that changing gaze. Both books, despite their very different aims, are also dealing with analytical spaces and how knowledge is shaped within those spaces. In his detailed discussion of *The Birth of the Clinic*, Gary Gutting (1989: 136) concludes that Foucault's 'analysis is a splendid instance of laying bare the a priori presuppositions involved in reports of allegedly uninterpreted data'. Instantly we can see how we might read across from *The Birth of the Clinic* to thinking about how data are understood, approached and interpreted today. The idea of 'allegedly uninterpreted data', as emphasised by Gutting, and the presumptions embedded in them remain powerful and relevant. It pushes us to reflect on the actors and industry that are invested in these a priori presuppositions that shape how data are seen and used.[2] As Foucault (1980: 146) put it in his own later reflections on the objectives of *The Birth of the Clinic*, he 'wanted to find out how the medical gaze was institutionalised, how it was effectively inscribed in social space, how the new form of the hospital was at once the effect and the support of a new type of gaze' (for a discussion of the privileging of the senses in Foucault's work see Jay, 1986: 176; or on the hierarchy of the senses see Bartkowski, 1988: 45). For Siisiäinen (2013: 26), the reason for the dominance of the eye in Foucault's account of the clinic is the capacity it provides to 'collect spatial facts or spatial data' (see also Nettleton, 1992: 94).

The Birth of the Clinic is a helpful conceptual resource for thinking about the questions I will attempt to address here, especially those concerning the role of expert knowledge in data capitalism, the emergence of analytical spaces and the discourse that accompanies these forms of knowledge. As a result, the book uses Foucault's *The Birth of the Clinic* to open up a series of questions about analytics and uses Foucault's conception of the clinical or medical gaze as inspiration for developing the concept of the *data gaze*.[3] Not only does the book use Foucault's arguments as a point of reference and frame from which its own conceptual arguments develop, it also uses Foucault's approach for inspiration. I tried to reflect on the type of documentary and archival work done by Foucault and then used this to ask what type of documents and archives can be used to explore this unfolding industry around data analytics.[4] Foucault's book led me to reflect on what type of resources are available and how they might be used to study data analytics. I have tried to think creatively about the archive and about documentary traces in this book. What I found was that there exists a massive amount of information, archived, that can be drawn upon for studying this type of topic. If we think laterally about archives and documents (see Allen-Robertson, 2017), there are numerable traces and accounts that can be pulled together to create insights. Rather than go into detail about this here, I will describe the materials gathered together in more detail in the individual chapters. In each case though, the archives and documents used are not the types that we might expect, but they represent entry points for gaining insights across this industry. I have called upon audio, visual and text-based accounts of practice, marketing materials, software protocols, project materials and guidelines, training and qualification materials, technical manuals and more traditional books and articles on developments in data and data work, amongst other sources.

Foucault's *The Birth of the Clinic* is a key influence, but what I find and argue here is quite different to the arguments made by Foucault. This book does not merely apply Foucault's work to the contemporary setting, nor is it a book about Foucault. Rather Foucault acts as a source of inspiration and provocation, his book provides a framework and set of ideas that are used to advance the arguments made here. In the hope of illuminating how data are seen, spoken through and articulated, I am putting Foucault's ideas to work. Foucault's gaze is just as useful for locating divergences as it is in highlighting resonances. The gaze adapts and mutates when deployed in the codified clinic of data analytics. Some key differences concern the spatiality and infrastructures of the gaze, the proximity and temporality of the gaze and most crucially I think, the notion of expertise and authenticity around who is able to deploy the gaze. Because of these differences, we cannot simply transpose Foucault's arguments about the clinic onto the unfolding forms of data-informed knowledge. The data gaze possesses a different kind of motivation, impulse, urgency and agenda to the 'clinical gaze' described by Foucault.[5] Yet a key aspect of the data gaze remains the idea that it can reveal hidden truths that are otherwise invisible. As we will see, it is often suggested that the data gaze is able to look into the blind-spots of the social world and illuminate the shadows.

In terms of structure, the book develops the concept of the data gaze by concentrating on and working through three focal points: *visions, infrastructures* and *practices*. First, the envisioning of data is explored in Chapters 2 and 3. These two chapters deal with what might be thought of as the *data imaginary*. These chapters look directly at the envisioning of data analytics and the rationalities that underpin those visions. Chapter 2 deals with the general features of the data imaginary, whilst Chapter 3 explores speed and acceleration as the most prominent aspects within this imaginary. The data imaginary is concerned with the promises, futures, potentials and possibilities that are associated with data. It is a concept that sensitises us to how data are envisioned. Chapters 2 and 3, together, explore the powerful ways in which data and analytics are presented and how this enables data-led processes, ordering and governance to spread and intensify. Chapters 2 and 3 set the scene and provide some overarching insights into the way that power is projected onto data analytics. The focus then shifts to data infrastructures. Chapter 4 focuses upon the analytical spaces of the data gaze – what we might think of as the *codified clinic*. It uses a case study of a particularly prominent and widely used software project, Hadoop, to explore the features of the data infrastructure and its transformations. The chapter starts with Hadoop but then explores the different components within data infrastructures to see how they are combined to create bespoke codified clinics for the data gaze to operate within. Finally, the book moves towards the practices of data analysis. This is perhaps the trickiest aspect, given the diversity of types of work and practice that fit into this broad field. Exploring the demarcation of a professional analyst and engineer, Chapter 5 looks at the division of roles within the analytics industry and how those roles are associated with different types of analytic gaze. This chapter looks at accounts of data analysis and engineering practices across this division of labour and looks at how expertise is associated with different adaptations of the data gaze. Collectively, these chapters explore how data are imagined, how infrastructures are engineered and how practices of analysis unfold. At the centre of each are the ways that the data gaze is constructed, deployed and realised.

These chapters represent the starting point of an analysis of an emergent industry and what appears, at the moment, to be an increasingly powerful set of actors, software and platforms that intermediate data-led processes allowing them to unfold, expand and deepen. The data gaze is explored in these chapters as a means for understanding how data intervene in the social and how data come to shape decisions, judgements and outcomes. To appreciate this requires an understanding of the intermediary roles being played – it is here that it is decided what those data say about us. The three steps taken in this book allow for an examination of how visions of data analysis are woven into infrastructures and practices.

The book may, on the surface, be dealing with a narrow industry. The key point here though is that data analytics reach out right across the social world. You might already find it hard to think of aspects of social life that go completely untouched by data analytics or that somehow reside outside of the scope of a data gaze. The book is not limited to the pursuit of an industry in its own right, but exists to think about how that industry is networked into social structures. It is intended to contribute something to an understanding of the structures in which we live and the forms of power that are in operation. Data analytics are almost always part of the operation of capitalism and should be seen through the lens of political economy (Beer, 2016b). The book has one eye on this broader context. Data capitalism or platform capitalism, if we might call it that, is the landscape that this book attempts to incorporate into the understanding of these analytics. Data analytics are, of course, a part of power structures, value generation and economic infrastructures. They should be approached with this in mind. The data gaze is where we can understand the formation of new forms of data-led knowledge and examine what these will mean. It is also where we can explore how data are seen and how we come to be seen, unendingly, through data.

NOTES

1. There are some connections between *The Birth of the Clinic* and Foucault's book on the author Raymond Rousel, which were both published in 1963. Foucault (1986) entitled one chapter 'The Empty Lens'. A small marker, perhaps, of a concern with the relations between knowledge, words and vision running across the two contemporaneous projects. The interest in the 'relationship of words to things' (Foucault, 1986: 130) or the 'dangerous twinkling of words and things' (Foucault, 1986: 153) echoes from the Rousel book into his other work on clinical medicine. Similarly, there is an underlying concern with the relations between visibility and invisibility that permeates into discussions of what is left out, what is seen, what is spoken and what is silent. Foucault reflects, for instance, upon the importance of what has been left out of Rousel's book *Nouvelles Impressions*. He concludes that 'Rousel has placed before our very eyes a pair of glasses whose lenses remain opaque' (Foucault, 1986: 125). The focal point is obscured leaving only the peripheral vision. This is in contrast with the descriptions elsewhere in which, Foucault observes, Rousel is capable of bringing the world into focus. The 'lens of the binoculars', he adds, holds the eye on details of nature on another occasion, and, foreshadowing the targeted glance described in *The Birth of the Clinic*, 'the eye looked through the lens and placed in the shadows anything that was not part of the spectacle' (Foucault, 1986: 132). The 'glance', Foucault (1986: 132) continues, 'pierced the glass lens, and the backdrop came sharply into focus'. The different lenses used in these descriptions of Rousel's prose seem to hold some pertinence for Foucault; it is not just what the lenses allow to be seen but how those lenses, through their framings and formulations, enable us to see more clearly or provide some sort of renewed focus. The role of the lens in clarifying and focusing was perhaps a preoccupation given the work that Foucault had also been doing on the history of the clinic and the role of the gaze in that environment.
2. Foucault's interest in the gaze was perhaps most famously developed in the third section of his classic 1975 text *Discipline and Punish* (see Foucault, 1991). It was in that book that Foucault's interest in the disciplinary power of the 'le regard' evolved (Jay, 1986: 181). But this obviously emerged from some earlier concerns. As O'Farrell (2005: 39) identifies:

    > The Key term that commentators and researchers have retained from *The Birth of the Clinic* is 'the gaze', a notion that resonates with Foucault's later popular idea of a society centred around surveillance … 'The gaze' at the end of the eighteenth century was aimed at revealing what had hitherto remained hidden and unseen not only in the physical body but also in the social and political body.

The notion of the gaze that he developed in *Discipline and Punish*, using Bentham's vision of the panopticon, has been widely adopted to think about questions of surveillance, social control and the disciplinary power of the potential to be watched. Of course, as has been frequently discussed, the panopticon was developed by Foucault into a concept that can be used to understand the ways that we internalise surveillance and discipline ourselves (Schwan and Shapiro, 2011: 127–39). It is also a concept that has been widely used to understand new media forms, big data, mobile devices and the like. The panopticon and variations on it have been important staples of the move towards understanding how power operates within decentralised media (see McMullan, 2015). I am hoping to do something a little different in this book, which is why I focus on the gaze as developed in *The Birth of the Clinic* and give less attention to that developed in Foucault's later work.

3. I am of course aware that this is not the only way in which the gaze has been conceptualised. In fact, the concept of the gaze takes us into some quite busy territory. It has been picked up and developed in lots of different ways, some of which have been highly influential and path-breaking (see for instance Sassatelli, 2011; Urry, 1990). Rather than providing an expansive overview and discussion of all of the various applications, I want to instead focus on a specific conceptualisation. Because this book is concerned with the relationship between the gaze and new types of emergent knowledge and analytics, I will focus predominantly upon Foucault's work on the emergence of the clinic. I am not intending to side-step what is a significant body of literature on how things are seen, looked at and observed. However, what I do aim to focus more centrally upon are the relationships between the gaze and the legitimation of knowledge. It is this aspect of the gaze that is most important to the questions I am asking here. In particular, this book is interested with how the gaze is facilitated and mobilised in relation to the formulation of knowledge, as well as the feedback between the two. For this reason and for the purpose of negotiating this tricky field, I settled on the conceptualisation of the gaze offered in Foucault's The Birth of the Clinic. Given my aims, I have chosen to work very closely with that particular conceptualisation of the gaze. This is not to disregard the literature on the gaze, but to focus on a particular angle so as to explore the aspect of the gaze that is most relevant.

4. I do not unpick the long-discussed properties, features and values of genealogical and archaeological approaches, this has been done extensively elsewhere. For examples of this see Dreyfus and Rabinow, 1982; During, 1992: 125–30; Gutting, 1994; O'Farrell, 2005: 64–9; Raffnsøe et al., 2016: 59–62.

5. It is worth noting at the outset that the concept of 'the gaze', 'the clinical gaze' or the 'medical gaze', is, in some respects at least, a product of the translation. Translated by A.M. Sheridan in 1973, the translator's note points out that the word 'gaze' was a choice made in the translation and is used where Foucault uses the French word *'regard'* (the exception being the book's subtitle where 'perception' is preferred). This choice may have implications for the concept itself . Tom Osborne (1992: 79) has commented on what this translation

might mean for how we understand and use Foucault's work; he points out that:

> The term certainly translates badly; 'the gaze' seems such an eccentric term in relation to the (presumably) more concrete (and philosophically resonant) *regard*. But if it is somehow the wrong word, this is not so much because it implies a subject who is 'gazing' – least of all an entirely unified subject whose gaze is the same at all times and all places – but because it is tied too closely to the act of vision. The notion of the gaze seems to privilege seeing. Whereas what is most fruitful about Foucault's actual usage of the term is that it is not simply a function of sight at all – or that, if it does indeed privilege the matter of sight, it includes other functions, such as speaking, touching, or knowing, as well.

The word gaze may well stand out as a concept more prominently than if the choice had been to translate '*regard*' as look, looking, seeing or perception or any other possibility. Also, Osborne points out that we might be incorrectly assuming that Foucault was privileging the gaze more than was actually the case. It is what we can do with the ideas and what possibilities they create that I am concerned with here. The initial intention of the meaning of the concept is perhaps less important than what it allows us to do once it is put to work and appropriated.

2

Envisioning the Power of Data Analytics: The Data Imaginary

Claims that data can answer our dreams of an ideal lifestyle/body/organisation/ performance/nation/future/economy/environment/other (delete as appropriate) are not hard to find. We are often confronted with such dreams. We are surrounded by powerful visions of what data can achieve, what they can solve, how they might help us to thrive, what they are able to reveal and how they are able to make us more informed, efficient or better at things. This might not even be something that we really notice, especially as the envisioning of the possibilities provided by data is both familiar and often neatly integrated into some particular issue or other. But what agendas underpin such dreamwork? What are these claims being used to achieve?

Dig a little deeper, beyond the popular media or beyond the types of analytics that pop up in news stories, documentaries, in our workplaces and so on, and you can begin to uncover just what type of power we imagine data to hold. It is often quite staggering. A new faith in data appears to have taken hold. It is by no means universal but it is a powerful and prevalent current. The answers we need, the solutions to some problem we might not even know that we had, are often thought to be somewhere in the data. It would seem that if only we had more data and more analytics we would know more and waste less. The data may hold some of these powers; I would suggest though that pausing to think about how data are imagined into existence can tell us a great deal. Implicit in these visions of data are variegated claims about the power of analytics. Although the talk is often of the data, it is actually the analytics that are seen to be powerful in realising their envisaged potential. These visions contain a range of compelling promises and possibilities, which are projected onto the data. Some of these promises may well be accurate, but let us put that notion of accuracy to one side for the time being and think about how the visions of data analytics are playing out and what they might be used to achieve. It is in this envisioning of the power of the data gaze, I would suggest, that a lot of work is being done to extend its reach and increase the responsibility placed upon data. To try to understand this role of the envisioning of data analytics, this chapter develops the concept of the *data imaginary*. The data imaginary is the data gaze's diamond tip, used for cutting, chipping, tearing and opening the spaces into which it can expand. As I will explain, the data imaginary is also a key part of how the data gaze is able to look upon data, and its properties become a kind of ever disappearing horizon that analytics infrastructures and practices pursue.

The dominant contemporary tropes about data, with their focus upon the influential social presence of *big* data, could easily distract us from the machinations of power that are at play. In many ways though, it is in these tropes, tucked within the rhetoric of the revolutionary potential of data analytics, that power is being exercised. It is here that the perceptions of the data are shaped and also where entry points are created for drawing data into social processes and prioritising their use in ordering and governing. These machinations underpin this chapter and spill into the chapters that follow. As the book proceeds, in the later chapters it explores how those visions weave into infrastructures and practices. Indeed, one of the arguments I will make in this particular chapter is that it is this ability to conjure such hype or 'cyberbole' (Woolgar, 2002) that is actually central to facilitating the spread of data-led practices. This is regarded as a key aspect of the data gaze, which is to say that its power is in fostering the appeal as well as promoting the authority of those types of knowledge. The sense that there is an overwhelming deluge of data today, however historically accurate this may be (see Beer, 2016b), means that when it comes to the so-called data revolution the power is firmly in the hands of those who are able to interpret or tell stories with the data (as outlined in Chapter 1). In short, the power of data is located in what they are used to reveal. For its power to expand it is necessary for the logic of the data gaze to become desirable – as well as for the infrastructures to emerge and the 'grids' (Foucault, 2003: 168) of the data gaze to be established. The data themselves come to life and begin to have consequences when they are analysed and when those analyses are integrated into social, governmental and organisational structures. This industry frames the data and projects possibilities and potential upon data analytics. The data analytics industry emphasises a particular vision of the social world so as to present data analytics as the only real solution. The power of data might well be located in what those data are used to reveal, but behind this power is an industry of activity working to spread those analytics and the optic horizons of the data gaze.

CREATING AND RESPONDING TO THE PROMISES OF DATA

It would appear that there has been a drastic escalation in the data available to organisations of various types (see Kitchin, 2014). As a result, the powerful intermediary role played by the analytics industry has taken on greater significance, as has their power to shape how data are understood and integrated into organisational life. Within notions of a 'data deluge' or a 'data revolution', we have tended to miss out these intermediaries and the role they play in realising the transformations towards data-intensive processes (as discussed in Chapter 1). Yet these intermediaries are central to both the conjuring of these visions of a deluge and the changes that those visions bring about. The mere fact that we talk of a data revolution compels us to imagine ways in which those data might be used. As we go about 'socialising big data' (Ruppert et al., 2015), we will need to bring these intermediaries into focus. This is to shift attention to the influential role that is played by those who are locating value, narrating and then attaching meanings to that data. Given that we know that these data are not 'raw' (Gitelman, 2013), we have perhaps paid too little attention to the data analyst and to the products and services of the data analytics industry. A powerful new assemblage of human and non-human actors now perform as *data intermediaries* within this apparently overwhelming accumulation of data. This particular chapter, as well as the one that immediately follows it, focuses directly on the visions of data analytics that are being put to work and which both frame and justify the data gaze.

As this might suggest, the analytics industry's role is varied and complex, not least because its actors are both creating *as well as* responding to these visions of data. As the availability of new types of data has grown and as the visions of a data deluge have been conjured in the powerful discourse of the data industry, the role of finding something comprehensible to say about this mass of accumulating data has taken on greater significance (as discussed in boyd and Crawford, 2012). If, as I have suggested, the power of data is in the insights that they are used to garner, then this data analytics industry is powerful in shaping what is said, made visible or known through data. It is crucial then to explore the growing analytical and interpretive power of this emergent industry as its reach spreads outwards, at different scales, across different social spheres.

It is not surprising that this industry of analytics, as we will see, positions itself as providing solutions to the data deluge. It provides, we are told, opportunities for anyone to see things with data. It provides services for a kind of data-led 'telling about society' (Becker, 2007) through, it is suggested, intuitive and accessible analytics packages. As such, the interpretive role of the data analytics industry now needs to take centre stage if we are to fully understand the way that power is exercised or deployed through data – ranging from larger to smaller scale providers. This chapter aims to illuminate the discourse that surrounds the analysis of data and show the powerful ways that the data analytics industry frames and projects analytical prowess. It is concerned with the way this industry cultivates a particular type of vision of data and their possibilities. The growing power of the data analytics industry, I suggest, is not just in what they do but in what they promise – in a similar way that expectations and promises play a central part in the 'dynamics' and 'momentum' of developments in science and technology (Brown and Michael, 2003). The allure and seductive envisioning of the possibilities of data is a key facilitator for the adoption, incorporation and spread of data-led processes. These visions, I suggest, can be seen as a part of the broader imaginary upon which organisational practice is based (see Knorr Cetina, 1994: 7–8).

THE POWER OF THE IMAGINARY

In his book *Modern Social Imaginaries*, Charles Taylor (2004) focuses upon the role played by 'social imaginaries'. He defines these as 'the ways people imagine their social existence, how things go on between them and their fellows, the expectations that are normally met, and the deeper normative notions and images that underlie these expectations' (Taylor, 2004: 23). The concept remains quite broad in Taylor's definition as he tries to capture the sense making and ordering potential of the imaginary. He separates this social imaginary from social theory by claiming that 'the social imaginary is that common understanding that makes possible common practices and a widely shared sense of legitimacy' (Taylor, 2004: 23). The social imaginary then is a projection of how things are. It is how the social is envisioned that enables common understanding and affords legitimacy.

This makes for a nuanced mix of properties. Taylor (2004: 24) argues that:

> ... our social imaginary at any given time is complex. It incorporates a sense of the normal expectations we have of each other, the kind of common understanding that enables us to carry out the collective practices that make up our social life. This incorporates some sense of how we all fit together in carrying out common practice. Such understanding is both factual and normative; that is, we have a sense of how things usually go, but this is interwoven with an idea of how they ought to go, of what missteps would invalidate the practice.

The social imaginary, for Taylor, has an integrated set of expectations and common understandings that make social practices possible. The result is that it carries norms and ideas about the world and what is valid. Part of how this works is that the social imaginary is imbued with ideals and ideal scenarios. Taylor (2004: 24) proposes that 'implicit in this understanding of the norms is the ability to recognize ideal cases ... And beyond the ideal stands some notion of a moral or metaphysical order, in the context of which the norms and ideals make sense'. The ideals that are woven into the social imaginary, Taylor is suggesting, are based upon and reinforce some moral order. It is the context provided by the social imaginary that means that these norms make sense. In short, the way things are imagined is powerful in defining ideals and norms. It is for this reason that this chapter explores the *data gaze* in combination with the concept of the *data imaginary*.

The social imaginary described by Taylor, as might be expected, interfaces with practice. What is envisioned shapes what is done. Taylor describes a kind of back and forth between the imaginary and practice. So, for instance, his claim is that:

> The relation between practices and the background understanding behind them is ... not one-sided. If the understanding makes the practice possible, it is also true that it is the practice that largely carries the understanding. (Taylor, 2004: 25)

The practice and the imaginary work on each other. As such, ideals and norms are forged as the imaginary is shaped in relation to practice and as practices respond to the imaginary. It seems that Taylor is suggesting that it is in this space that the social imaginary can adapt and change. As Taylor then writes, 'what is originally just an idealization grows into a complex imaginary through being taken up and associated with social practices' (Taylor, 2004: 29). Starting as an ideal or a theory, these ideas grow as they mix into practice and become established – reshaping the social imaginary and affording a 'new outlook' that makes sense of practices and begins to define 'the contours of their world' (Taylor, 2004: 29). It is this shaping of the contours of the world that has led Taina Bucher (2017), reflecting on the way that social media are experienced, to develop the idea that there is an 'algorithmic imaginary' at play within these media, especially as Facebook's algorithms' 'ordinary affects' are experienced. The point here is that the data imaginary is also caught in a back and forth between vision and practice. In some cases this back and forth is being engineered to enframe certain practices. The power of these visions is actively used in order to take practice in a certain direction and to move towards increased and intensified data analytics. Intervening in the social imaginary, or the data imaginary, can spiral this back and forth in certain directions. There is undoubtedly, as it has been described, a 'politics of imagination' (Bottici, 2012).

This broader concept of social imaginaries can be used as a platform for understanding the data imaginary that I discuss in this and the following chapter. The data imaginary can be understood to be part of how people imagine data and its existence, as well as how it is imagined to fit with norms, expectations, social processes, transformations and ordering. The data imaginary is about how data are imagined in the social world and how they intervene in the connections between people and between people and organisations, nation states, media and their material environment. There are ideals and norms bound up with data within this imaginary. The data imaginary in this way is part of the broader social imaginary, a kind of component within it: it is part of how we imagine data within the broader ways that we imagine the social. A key aspect of what this chapter does though is not just take the data imaginary as a common set of understandings, rather it is looking at how that imaginary is cultivated and fostered as part of a set of commercial agendas and driven by an interest in shaping common understandings and founding the legitimacy of data-led practices.

As this indicates, this particular chapter focuses very specifically upon the way in which data and data analytics are envisioned within the rhetoric of the data analytics industry. It is argued here that to understand the spread of data analytics and the adoption of certain analytic strategies, we first need to look at the projection of promises upon those data. The way that data and analytics are imagined shape their incorporation and appropriation into practices and organisational structures – what I call here *data frontiers*. The data imaginary is being designed to reduce the resistances at these data frontiers and create gaps for the data gaze to occupy. This and the following chapter draw upon a sample of 34 data analytics companies in order to explore the way in which data analytics are envisioned within that increasingly powerful industry.

The key argument of this chapter is that the data imaginary is central to the framing and spread of analytic processes. Using the public marketing materials from these 34 data analytics companies (for the full list see the Appendix), this chapter explores how data analytics are imagined or envisioned across the sector. As I have suggested, taking such an approach enables us to understand *the conceptual making-up of data and data analytics*. The point here is that the promises that are being made, act as incentives to the expansion of 'datafication' (van Dijck, 2014). *Data frontiers*, as I call them, are the edges, thresholds and limits of data led-processes. It is at these edges or frontiers where the visions are most active in trying to shove back those boundaries. The data imaginary that I will describe is most active at the data frontiers, at the boundary lines at which data-informed processes reach their limits. Data frontiers are what we might think of as the limits of datafication. Those invested in this industry are inevitably seeking to push these boundaries back. It is at these frontiers that these visions of the power of data analytics do their work. They are active in ushering in the expansion and intensification of data within organisational and social structures. These visions of data analytics persuade, enact and produce notions and ideals that are designed to force back those frontiers. If we are to understand the expansion and intensification of data as an active component of the social world, then we need to look at the work that is being done at these data frontiers.

Yet data frontiers are not simple boundary lines; rather these frontiers work in two ways. First we have the entry of data analytics into previously uncharted and new territories. These are social territories into which data analytics are yet to spread. And, second, we have frontiers at which data are already active but where the usage is relatively limited or basic. In these territories, there is the pursuit of the further enhancement and escalation of those data processes.

These are frontiers where data have seeped in but the deluge has been held back. Hence these data frontiers are sites of attempted expansion *and* intensification. The more powerful the envisioning of the data analytics then, the more porous these data frontiers are likely to be. These boundaries may be a product of a reticence or resistance towards data analytics, or they may be a result of a lack of resources or the stubbornness of obdurate social processes and practices. The data imaginary, as we will see, is designed to overcome such blockages. Of course, this is not to say that these visions of the power of data analytics will always equate directly to the realities of organisational data use, but it is to say that these visions will feed into those organisational practices, perceptions and structures (some of which we will explore in Chapters 4 and 5). We need to see the promises that are being made in order to understand how these particular types of data analysis, and the thinking behind them, work their way into the structures in which we live. Or as Ien Ang (1985: 83) famously put it, admittedly in a very different context, 'a life without imagination does not exist'.

LOCATING THE DATA ANALYTICS INDUSTRY

The aims of this chapter (and also Chapter 3) required the identification of a series of data analytics organisations whose activities could then be examined. The sample was created by first searching for three different combinations of terms. Google was used as it was imagined that this is likely to be where organisations start when they are looking for analytics expertise. The search terms used were: (1) data analytics companies; (2) data analytics organisations; (3) data analytics solutions. These were felt to be the most appropriate terms and were also felt to be representative of the type of terms organisations might use when trying to locate data analytics services. The sample was then created using search terms 1 and 3. These two terms produced the most useful and extensive lists of the type of organisations that were being sought. Two different approaches were then used to create a list of organisations that varied in type. The top 10 results for search term 1 included two recent magazine articles that provided overviews of a range of data analytics companies. *Network World*[1] and *Forbes*[2] magazines had published articles on big data companies 'to watch'. These lists were used to create a list of data analytics companies that were in some way notable in the industry. I used these two magazine lists, visiting the websites of the named analytics companies and including within my sample any companies that described themselves as providing data analytics (see Appendix). It was recognised that some supplementary examples beyond those contained in the magazine articles were needed. I used search term 3 to locate a further six data analytics providers. To do this I simply selected the first six companies that were listed in my Google search that in some way identified themselves as providing data analytics (excluding those that had already been included in my sample as a result of being named in one of the magazine lists). This created a sample of 34 data analytics organisations of different types, ranging from consultancy to software package providers.[3] The sample of data analytics organisations is listed in the Appendix. The Appendix also contains some further information about the sample (I will also add some further detail about market position and market share in Chapter 3).

Once the sample had been established, I then explored the marketing materials as published on the public websites of each of the organisations in the sample. In each case, and in line with the aims of this chapter, I looked specifically for instances in which the data analytics services provided were being described, rather than any other types of services. This enabled me to focus specifically upon how these data analytics were being presented in the materials provided by each company. As well as focusing upon content concerning data analytics, I looked for three more specific things to help to guide the analysis. First, I looked at the types of services and solutions that were on offer. This step was used to explore the different types of data analytics that were being presented and to see what types of problems or opportunities these solutions were said to be offering. Second, I looked at the scale and scope of those services and solutions. That is to say that I looked at the size of opportunities that were presented, the notions of scale that were being discussed, the inclusion of any geography or size of data set and the type of coverage that was being offered. Third and finally, I also focused attention on the promises, hopes and expectations that were linked to the data and its analysis: What was it said that they offer? What changes and transformations were data analytics said to bring about? These were the key points of focus that were used to navigate the resources and provide some direction in extracting materials that spoke to the core aims of this project.

THE DATA IMAGINARY

From exploring the materials in the way described above, a number of themes occurred frequently in the content. Six themes were found to have particular prominence in the materials. Each theme emphasises a particular property or feature of data analytics. This is, of course, to be expected. We are looking here at marketing materials. We would expect them to attempt to sell the features and benefits of data analytics to an imagined customer. To reiterate my earlier point though, this requires us to see this not simply as an exercise in promotion but as a series of attempts to instigate, facilitate and afford the expansion of data-led processes of evaluation, judgement and decision making. This is the rhetoric aimed at oiling the spread of data and the type of calculative judgements, ordering and evaluation that it brings. Seeing the detail of how data analytics are constructed in sales pitches to organisations helps in understanding more clearly how these analytics spread across sectors, how they are understood and in what form they come to embed themselves in our everyday lives.

What emerged was a very specific *data imaginary* in which data analytics are presented as *speedy, accessible, revealing, panoramic, prophetic* and *smart*. The rest of the chapter explores the details of each of these features of this data imaginary.

SPEEDY

If there is one overriding message of the visions conjured by this set of materials, it is that data and data analytics are speedy, quick, fast or rapid. They do not hang around dwelling over possible insights, they are instant and continuous. We are told that they allow organisations to respond to their data in 'real-time'. Thus these are data analytics that allow the analyst, in its broadest sense, to be *in the moment* and to react without delay or hesitation to the changing scenes that they see unfolding. This is data mobility in real-time. The insights produced by the data are seen to be a representation of the world as it unfolds – rather than being a reflective process of looking back. There is no delay or gap in the knowledge being produced, rather these data analytics are depicted as providing continuous encounters with the actually existing world as it is in that moment. This, of course, recalls the immediacy of the gaze (which I return to in the following chapter).

There is an interesting temporality at play in these visions of data analytics. The data produces insights into those moments, but this is also an ongoing and continuous process. The vision is of an always switched-on presence of analytics in the background, leading to moments of punctuation in which a response, decision or reaction is needed. The quicker the analytics, so the logic goes, the better and more useful it is. Quick analytics lead to responsive, flexible and successful organisations, it is implied – as is fitting with the prominent notions of organisational and worker agility discussed recently by Phoebe Moore (2018).

Part of this speed is tied into the envisioning of the power of these analytics. These are presented as being an invitation to 'supercharge'[4] or 'turbocharge'[5] your analytics. These analytics are not only described as fast, they are also powerful or mighty – the sense is of them having horse-power under the bonnet. The use of engine metaphors is telling here, with the analytics machine being like a souped-up high-performance engine, with extra power, torque and superior revolutions per minute – at least that is what is conveyed. The usual 'metaphors of big data' (Puschmann and Burgess, 2014), as they have been described, are never far away.

The result is an intensive form of knowledge that arrives in real-time … continuously. This runs in parallel with broader notions of a kind of jam-packed, inescapable and real-time experience of 'intensive culture' (Lash, 2010). A flow of knowledge and insights gushes, yet the complexity of the data is simplified to enable their quick and rapid usefulness. This is to quickly find accurate insights without hesitation, despite the massive deluge. As is illustrated by the passages suggesting that this is a kind of 'speed at scale'[6] there are a number of references to such claims[7]. Again, we see assertions about the speediness with which insights are drawn from the huge accumulating data as they are harvested, enabling a quick response. In another instance this is described as closing the gap between the gathering of data and its use in making decisions: 'achieve rapid insight into action across your organisation, closing the gap between transactions, data preparation, analysis, and action – all with analytics'[8]. Closing this gap is seen to be an acceleration of the working practices of organisations, who are then able to react nimbly and instantly to those insights – with there being no gaping fissure between data capture and analysis. I will discuss this 'closing of the gap' in much more detail in the following chapter, where I will also discuss the implied combination of scale or volume with the speed of analytical insights.

Taken together, these 34 examples describe speedy analytics in which masses of data can continuously be drawn upon to inform and enlighten organisational processes and decision making. The image is of a more intensive organisation that reacts to real-time knowledge about itself. The gap between data and knowledge is depicted as closing. These are speedily accumulating data that are rapidly analysed. Such claims represent attempts to provide solutions that cope with broader notions of cultural speed-up and acceleration (as discussed by Tomlinson, 2007; Wajcman, 2015). The idea is that companies that use data analytics can accelerate their practices and keep up with what is perceived to be an accelerating world and set of competitors.

As I have indicated, the focus on speed is a key aspect of the data imaginary and of how the products and services of the data analytics industry are imagined. Having introduced this particularly prominent feature here, I intend to develop it much further in the following chapter. The entanglement of speed and acceleration with data is crucial to understanding the promises projected onto data analytics; unpicking this requires a dedicated and more detailed discussion. As such, Chapter 3 explores this aspect of the data imaginary in much more detail. Speed is the most pressing and dominant of the features, so has been given the extra treatment.

ACCESSIBLE

Alongside speed, the accessibility of these analytics is a second key theme. A dominant idea here is that knowledge can be gleaned without any real technical know-how. Thus these are instant analytics both in the sense that the data analytics produce instant results and in the sense that users can readily interpret and understand the analytics that they are encountering. The data might be incomprehensible but the analytics are intuitive and can therefore be easily accessed and understood. The software is doing the work for you. The software provides the analyses from which *anyone* can draw inference. Thus the data are rendered accessible and their analysis requires little training or expertise. The software becomes the expert intermediary in the data analysis relationship that is being envisioned here. The growing role of the expert and the consultant has been noted in some important recent contributions (Amoore, 2013: 6; Davies, 2014: 30); I pick up again on some of these themes in Chapter 5. The message conveyed in these marketing materials though is that you can become your own expert and consultant, with the help of these easy-to-use, proactive and intuitive software packages. The software, it is claimed, turns the user into a data analyst.

Simplification of complexity is the key underlying message. They are products and services designed to make your data accessible, with the words ease, easy and easily appearing frequently. The visualisation of data is one particular area of focus in the accessibility of the data.[9] Ideas and theories are then tested and reworked in these processes of visualisation. Here the work being done by the visualisation (see Kennedy et al., 2016) is to render data amenable to instant and simplified analytical insights that are manageable by anyone. These visualisations are presented as being a translational device for enabling the untrained eye to easily extract knowledge from the data. The visualisations are presented as being one means by which these devices are making data manageable, comprehensible and instant. Again, this is seen to be part of the bypassing of technical skill. To communicate this type of empowerment and accessibility, terms like 'self-service'[10] and 'do-it-yourself'[11] are frequently used. Becoming an analyst and taking on these self-service software enables the user to 'take control of your data'[12]. This suggests that these are solutions that enable organisations to engage in their own data analytics so as to empower them in their data usage. These are data analytics then that are designed to give the impression of bypassing the expert third party and are instead about making everyone their own data analytics specialist. The industry of analytics appears to be premised upon its ability to turn anyone into a data analyst with their own data gaze.

In terms of access, what we have here is something close to what Steve Graham (2004a, 2004b) has called the 'dreams of transcendence' or the 'any-thing-anywhere-anytime-dream'. This is most directly articulated in the claim: 'Your business is changing and you need an easy, visual way to explore your data … [this] enables you to analyze any data, anytime, anywhere'[13]. The data analytics then are seen to be accessible at anytime or from anywhere, thus the temporality and spatiality of data analytics are not anchored to organisational buildings or to fixed working hours. The analytics are accessible both in terms of time and space. The analytics are 'all in one place'[14], with everything reduced to a single package. As Chapter 4 will show, these analytics may be located in one place but this place is mobile and transient.

REVEALING

Similarly, trust is an issue in the coverage of the insights that the data are said to offer. Unsurprisingly, the insights are depicted as being trustworthy and accurate. There is a promotion of what Theodor Porter (1995) has referred to as a 'faith' or 'trust' in numbers. Data analytics are presented as being about objectivity and efficiency in the production of insights (see Beer, 2016b). These revelations are said to be limitless in their flexibility, there are no boundaries to data or to what they facilitate for organisations.

The implicit theme here is that there is a raft of untapped potential to be found in the data; it is this potential that can be unlocked through analytics. Analytics are presented as being the means by which 'hidden'[15] value might be unearthed or where new types of value might be tapped. As it is put in one instance, there is a potential 'gold mine'[16] of information. As Foucault argued, in relation to the clinical gaze, 'the clinic no longer has simply to read the visible; it has to discover its secrets' (Foucault, 2003: 148). This data gaze is similarly about creating or extracting the hidden features. In the case of the data gaze, the focus is on locating the secrets of value. The images are of masses of wasted unused data that could be potentially lucrative. The analytics packages and solutions are said to provide opportunities to salvage this unused data waste.

The revelations are not seen to end here though. Rather, tapping into these hidden insights is said to provoke the newly informed analyst to ask new questions and seek insights. Again, as with the notion of self-service, these analytics packages are seen to provide opportunities for self-training and for radical culture-shifts within organisations (I return to this in Chapter 5). This is about organisations being charged with taking control of their data. The suggestion is that the insights produced will motivate and inspire those who use it to seek more and more analytical insights and to ask new questions about their organisations. These analytics, then, are designed for the 'curious'[17], those who want to 'look closely at what others ignore'[18] or who want to 'solve really hard problems'[19]. In this vision the analytics take on a performative role that goes beyond their function and which is about the reshaping of cognition and practice. It is being suggested that the analytics will make you think differently and provoke a new desire to learn. It is claimed that the analytics will provoke or stimulate 'curiosity'[20]. Data analytics, in this formulation, are said to breed and satisfy curiosity and the pursuit of hidden value. This then is an invitation to dig, packaged with the motivation to do so. As such, the impression or connotation is that these data analytics, far from producing passivity, will make the user less dependent on others for understanding – with new activities and ways of thinking burgeoning from those revelations.

PANORAMIC

As might then be expected, these data analytics are depicted as being all-seeing. They offer a kind of prosthetic eye with which to see the data that are accumulating. Data analytics are presented as almost omnipotent. They are inescapable and comprehensive in their scope, vision and sight. Nothing escapes this prostheticised and technologically enhanced vision. This is a gaze removed from the analytical spaces of the clinic and which can see everywhere. These data analytics, it is suggested, allow their user to 'see around corners and into the future'[21]. In other words, there is nowhere to hide from their gaze. Data analytics shine a light on blind-spots: those parts of the organisation hidden around corners suddenly become visible. Nothing is in the shadows. Pushing a similar set of ideas, data analytics are said elsewhere to provide a '360-degree view'[22]. Hence data analytics are described as having a kind of panoramic view in which nothing is outside of the knowledge that is produced from the data. Despite the scale and density of the data, the view from that position is comprehensive. Having masses of material to look at, it seems, does not provide a distraction or obstacle to the view. A variety of terms are used to account for the way that the whole is – or the many parts are – made visible in this way. It would seem that by bringing together different forms of data these analytics are able to expand the scope of their sight (see Chapter 4). The focus here is upon the ability to draw together different data streams in order to increase the coverage of the analytics. In this regard terms like 'integrated' or 'integration'[23], 'blending'[24], and 'harmonization'[25] are used to suggest the seamless use of variegated data to produce a coherent and comprehensive set of insights. This vision may be panoramic in scope, but as with the relation between the gaze and the glance (Foucault, 2003: 149), it can also be targeted (I return to this issue of the glance in the following chapter). This glance is captured in claims such as: 'Sift through any data using visual analytic tools. Pinpoint what matters, then put together a story of your data-driven conclusion'[26]. With the gaze being envisioned here, there is oversight which enables the features deemed important to be identified and focused in upon.

A big part of the claims being made is that this panoramic view affords insights into things that were previously outside of our field of vision. The result is that hidden value can be extracted from the depths of the structures in which we live.[27] Take this excerpt for example:

> If you're like most business people, you invest in data analytics to uncover hidden connections, unseen correlations, unknown customer preferences, and other useful information. Maybe you want to make better decisions about which products and services will delight customers, or perhaps you want to uncover process changes that could cut costs and shorten time to market.[28]

The data imaginary is premised upon a growing ability to see the unseen. To illuminate the hidden connections. To see below the surface and into the darkness. The result, it is suggested, is that this sight bestows better judgement. This is what happens, according to this data imaginary, when you are able to 'visualize the data from every angle'[29]. Not only can the data be used to see everywhere, there is also a push to see everything in terms of its data. As it is put in one instance, 'we see data – everywhere'[30]. As described above, this is said to breed curiosity, with the emphasis then placed upon the idea that these analytics allow people to see things that others cannot see. As it was put in one instance, 'it enables the curious to look closely at what others ignore – machine data – and find what others never see: insights that can help make your company more productive, profitable, competitive and secure'[31]. The data gaze, within this imaginary, is founded upon the idea that the beholder can see things that others will never see. It is the curious who seek out the data gaze and who develop this type of sight. This ability to see across, to 'spot trends, anticipate behavior, and ultimately, take action', it is claimed, 'is for people who are curious about data, want to solve really hard problems'[32]. This idea of curious puzzle solvers is something we will return to in Chapter 5.

As well as providing a panoramic view of the internal workings of organisations, these data analytics are also described as providing a perfect panoramic view of the exterior context. The organisation using these analytics is then able to fully understand their position within the world of capitalist competition. This external panorama is constructed through the data, so that the organisation might make use of its position and the new insights into its global competitors. The emphasis is upon the use of international data through which such analyses can be performed, and through which comparative forms of understanding might develop. The emphasis here is upon data analytics turning companies into world-players, or to enhance their position on the world stage. This is to take advantage of what is described as 'this hyper-connected world, with data volumes constantly increasing'[33]. Another instance is the observation that 'the world runs on data'[34]. The result is that data analytics allow for this context to be drawn upon to 'explore the world's public data'[35]. Data analytics then are envisioned as providing a panoramic view of the interior and exterior world.

PROPHETIC

It might be expected that notions of the future are important in data analytics, particularly where anticipation and prediction are often seen to be powerful in affording decision making and judgement. The data imaginary is founded upon an ability to grasp the future and use it in the present. To illustrate this point, one example of this is to be found in such claims as 'the next generation of analytics will let you see patterns for predicting future behaviors, not just analyzing those in the past'[36]. The data gaze, it would seem, has both sight *and* foresight.

The visibility provided by data analytics, as has already been hinted, is not just about the moment in which it occurs. They are said to act in real-time and provide a comprehensive view of the internal and external conditions; beyond this these data analytics are also said to have prophetic properties. Data analytics, in this imaginary, open up a world in which it is possible to anticipate what will happen, and respond accordingly. Such anticipation, embodied in the desire to use imagined futures to inform decisions, reflects what Louise Amoore (2013) has called 'the politics of possibility'. The way those futures are imagined clearly has important implications for what happens in the present, especially as those potential futures begin to mix into the present moment. Amoore's key point is that the sight we have of future scenarios has consequences and outcomes once those horizons are used to anticipate and predict outcomes. Clearly data analytics are complicit in such imagined futures, meaning that there is a politics to the anticipation they are said to afford. As well as providing a vision of the moment in real-time, data analytics are imagined as strategic and as having an eye on the future. In their promotion, a key value is in the ability of data analytics to provide a window onto the future, seeing into the future to protect and maintain value and a competitive edge. They enable the spotting of trends, with real-time data used to infer futures – meaning the user, in this imaginary, can anticipate rather than respond. Whereas Espeland and Sauder (2007) speak of 'reactivity' to data, where we change our behaviours in response to the data being gathered, here we see anticipation being ramped up and reactivity being folded into imagined futures.

A further underlying narrative here is that data analytics are a necessity for progress. It is what intelligent forward thinking organisations are seen to do – data analytics are conjured as being the desirable direction for all organisations. They aim to predict, forecast and bring the future into the present. This change is even described as being part of a 'New industrial revolution'[37], which we might interpret as a suggestion that there is a marked epochal change brought about by data and their analyses. A key aspect of this is obviously the stated ability to predict behaviours. As it was put in one instance, 'the next generation of analytics will let you see patterns for predicting future behaviors, not just analyzing those in the past'[38]. Seeing patterns and making predictions are a key part of these messages. Not just seeing the past but also then using patterns to see the future.

These pitches emphasise the need for a clear sense of the future along with the flexibility to respond to current changes. Or as it is put in one case: 'Future-proof your organization without ever getting locked in'[39]. Being able to predict the future is seen to be of extreme value in remaining responsive. The analytics industry draws in potential customers with provocative leading questions such as: 'What if you could accurately predict your customer's behavior?'[40]. The idea is that by predicting you are able to anticipate what people will want and shape your business accordingly, thus protecting its future value. The emphasis here is upon visions of strategic and intelligent thinking – a kind of predictive intelligence emerges in this rhetoric. For example, one package is said to provide 'predictive intelligence to help your agents be more productive and focus where customers need them most'[41]. Prediction and predictive intelligence, or so it is conveyed, enable enhanced value extraction. In another instance this is described as 'deep predictive analytics'[42]. Indeed, this seems to be an attempt to go beyond the frequently mentioned 'predictive analytics'[43], so as to suggest that there is a depth to the insights that might be generated by the 'predictive capabilities'[44] of these data analytics. The objective of the gaze described by Foucault, in very broad terms, is to try to make the invisible visible, to make the unseen seen. Foucault (2003: xxi) talks of this process of exploring the depths and volumes in a number of ways. In some instances it is a process of making the unseen seen. Here we have the gaze exploring the depths so as to bring things to the surface. Making visible is volumetric, it requires seeking insights that reside below the surface and below the usual level of perception. This observation below the level of perception is a crucial feature. The pursuit of vertical explorations of depths and volume remains at the centre of this version of the gaze.

As this demonstrates, data analytics are presented not just as enabling future sight, they also bring those desired futures into existence. Data become the producers and enablers of futures and outcomes. This then is about using data to see and then manipulate possible futures through current action and decisions. It is about making decisions informed by those imagined futures. The implicit logic of adapting and incorporating such methods is that it is the best or only way to remain competitive and to ensure a safe future. The imperative is to get ahead of the game. Without such analytic expertise the impression is that the result will be an inevitable decline as you fall behind the pack. The analytics industry is built upon this idea that data should be used to your advantage, whilst also being backed up by the idea that missing out on data will lead to a failure of vision. Thus companies are told that they need comprehensive and holistic analytics that capture everything, or 'an end to end data solution'[45], to facilitate data-led decision making that is positioned as better and more forward-thinking. Dreams of predictive intelligence are wrapped up in an ability to anticipate the future. This is a kind of future that is to be made real by data.

SMART

The above shows that the predictive capacities of data analytics are often associated with a latent intelligence that resides in these systems. Smartness, artificial intelligence and machine learning, which are widely discussed topics of debate, are inevitably a part of how these systems are described. Often the idea is that they can learn in order to predict. The notion of learning is important here. The analytics are not passive, rather they are presented as being intelligent and active devices that are able to learn, adapt and develop in the insights that they produce. They are also depicted as being able to respond to the user and to learn what they need in their analysis. A picture of a powerful intelligence emerges. They respond to particular needs, learning what is required, whilst also learning from the data that are accumulating.

Indeed, the word 'smart' is used a good deal to evoke this latent intelligence and learning power. This deals with both the smartness of the analytics and the smartness of the insights that they create – and then the implied and inherited smartness of the individuals or organisations that use them. For instance, we are told that these analytics bring 'Smarter answers to big data questions'[46] and 'Better Analytics, Smarter Decisions'[47]. A big part of the smartness described is associated with the type of 'machine learning' or 'machine intelligence' that resides within these analytics packages. With one claiming that it:

> ... deploys world-class machine learning algorithms to help you predict your customer's monetary value. Our proprietary algorithms are self-learning so they automatically improve and adjust throughout your customer's lifetime.[48]

Here the algorithms take on the thinking, with the analytics being based on forms of machine learning. These algorithms do not need training, it is implied, rather they do the learning for themselves, they are a 'self-learning' technology that is able to adjust to its own discoveries. This is said to create improved results, as it is put in one instance: 'Machine intelligence delivers better outcomes'[49]. Again there are connotations of progress woven into this, that data analytics provide the only sensible future for social ordering, governance and decision making processes. Also there is the connotation that the thinking, the difficult work of the analytics, can be done by the analytics software. This reinforces those earlier notions of accessibility, with the self-training algorithms helping to provide the self-service analytics to the untrained user. The software is training itself so that the interested user does not need to. This creates a set of questions around agency, with the data analytics software often seen to be doing much of the thinking, which relates to debates about the relations between data and agency (see Kennedy et al., 2015).

Indeed, the theme of self-learning and machine intelligence are woven through many of the instances in this sample. The data analytics are seen to learn about the data and the demands of their users. We get claims that the analytics are: 'backed by self-learning algorithms that tune for actual heavy query patterns'[50] or 'Advanced machine learning algorithms learn as you go, allowing you to focus on insights'[51]. In this second instance, we see again the point that the software does the analytical thinking so that the human actor is able to focus on the outputs of those analytics. Again, little technical knowledge is needed. This is presented as 'out-of-the-box Artificial Intelligence tools'[52]. There is, it is said, 'built-in intelligent data inferencing'[53]. The image is of ready-made and thinking technologies that carry the burden of technique, know-how and method. It is ready to do the thinking for you.

The consequence of this is that these thinking technologies are seen to find and locate value in a way that the human alone is unable to do. As this passage illustrates, the claim is that a particular analytics package 'leverages advanced machine learning algorithms to create significant business value and insights correlating internal and external data for any Enterprise'[54]. This type of 'machine learning'[55], is used to find value through algorithmic means. The algorithms are depicted here as active, autonomous and learning components within the software. The algorithms are described as being the means by which this learning takes place and are able to adapt to the data and to the types of insights that are desired. The software package is not then a complete product, rather it is presented as an organic system that actively evolves in its powers over time. As this instance suggests: 'Our proprietary algorithms are self-learning so they automatically improve and adjust throughout your customer's lifetime'[56]. This image is of a responsive and changing technology that hones its own analytics. This 'self-Learning' means that these packages 'update continuously without manual intervention'[57]. The result, it is suggested, is 'blending machine learning with human intelligence'[58]. It is not that humans are cut out of the equation, rather they work alongside these thinking technologies. These are presented as 'an intelligence engine that uncovers hidden insights in data and supports automated decision making'[59]. This automation does not mean that the human actors are described as passive. Rather, frequently, the learning and thinking analytics are presented as an aid to human decision making. Human and machine agency seem to be able to blend into some kind of harmony. The software even takes on a kind of anthropomorphic presence, making this blending less of a leap and again emphasising the intuitiveness – as is demonstrated by the idea that 'their experience feels less like it was produced by a machine, and more like it's coming from a friend'[60]. In this case the suggestion is that the interactions between human and machine are facilitated and made seamless by the machine behaving like a human presence. More than this, the learning system is said to be comfortable in its relations, like a friend. The result is that these new forms of agency or intelligence in machine learning and algorithms are presented in terms of their ability to complement, extend and blend with human agency.

CONCLUSION

Although I have predominantly focused upon the textual accounts provided by the sample I created, the materials I gathered were full of audio-visual presentations of data and data analytics. Many of the providers have short films to accompany their analytic products and services. Frequently these visions take on the form of a kind of disembodied and rapid depiction of dashboards, graphs and visualisations. These slick and instant dashboards populate the screens of different size devices from tablet computers to phones and desktops. Rhythmic music pulses as an enthused business-like voice tells of the properties of the services and software. Perhaps unsurprisingly, these films echo the properties of the data imaginary discussed in the previous pages. Slick in their delivery, clean and unencumbered by active human bodies, these short films focus on the data and the analytics. The rapid movements between images suggest something of the instantaneous and intuitive way that they allow data to be utilised. The photographs and other images used tend to follow a pattern: with the photographs sometimes showing people happily or efficiently hovering over devices, thinking, pointing, often huddled around a screen or screens collaborating. On other occasions they are shown out-and-about analysing their data whilst moving through or resting in public settings. In some cases overhead city shots, industrial settings and maps are used to emphasise the role of data in logistics, planning and distribution. The logistical visions act as a reminder of the message that data have material possibilities and are a transformative social presence. In other cases the calmness of nature is introduced in landscape photos of mountainscapes, fields or rivers. Here the flow, fluid and liquid metaphors find a visual dimension. All of these visual encounters fit with the type of accounts described in this chapter. Despite exploring them in my background research – therefore shaping the features I drew from these sources – I have not focused on these films and images in detail here, but they do suggest themselves as being a ripe ground for further analysis of this data imaginary.

This chapter has looked at the rolling-out of a logic, a way of thinking. As I have outlined, a very particular rationality emerges here – a rationality that promotes quick and accessible know-how that enables all-seeing predictive and smart decision making. It is a world in which anyone can be their own data analyst. These are powerful promises that are active in shaping and pushing back *data frontiers* – expanding both the reach and intensity of data-led processes. The logic is hard to resist. Who would not want to follow the logic of the six characteristics of the data imaginary that I have pulled out? The seductive allure becomes clear to see; it also begins to suggest how these characteristics might become a part of how data analytics are subsequently folded into organisations. The emergent industry of data analytics – providing both solutions and a compelling rationale – is powerful in its intermediary role. It is an industry built upon the idea that the accumulation of data needs a response, and that the only logical response is to use as many data as possible.

This data imaginary, I would suggest, is complicit in configuring the 'new data relations' (Kennedy, 2016: 232) and in the rise of the new 'data intermediaries' (Schrock and Shaffer, 2017). The data imaginary is an active part of the assemblage of human actors, code, software and algorithms that shape the circulation and integration of new forms of data. These data intermediaries are active in building the infrastructures central to what Pasquale (2015) has called the 'black box society' – a society with a range of underpinning algorithmic processes in which we have little knowledge or understanding of the secrets it holds or the knowledge it obfuscates. This chapter has looked at the distracting shiny veneer that is polished onto Pasquale's 'black box society'. The power of the data analytics industry is not just to be found in what it helps organisations to know or say with their data. Rather, a significant part of the power of the data analytics industry is in how it actively and enthusiastically envisions data and data analytics. It is here that data gain their edge, drawing people in. It is here that data analytics are presented as a competitive necessity. It is here that data analytics are imagined and thus where their incorporation is instigated. So, it is not enough to say that data analytics are being sold in this marketing rhetoric; rather we need to look at the detail of exactly how data and data analytics are being made up in this marketing speak. The power of the data analytics industry is two-fold: it is to be found in both the way that the data analytics are envisioned as well as in the actual data solutions that are then deployed on the ground. Without the former, we do not have the latter. It is the compelling rationale that ushers in these practices and carves spaces for expanding the scope and intensity of the data gaze.

The data analytics industry is inevitably attempting to theorise and imagine a future that potential customers will be seduced by. The result is that it conjures up a range of possible futures for those organisations so as to pull them into datafication. The shock of the new is tempered by reassuring images of a successful and desirable future and a forward-looking organisational way of life. Data and their analyses are presented as being a powerful, ongoing and permanent presence, giving constant insights that are always there. Those insights are then readily available in easy-to-consume forms that require little technical expertise – leading to judgement without know-how. These analytics reveal hidden value in the data, they shine a light on organisations and show things that were previously invisible. They enable the future to be seen and an imagined future to be part of the present decisions that are taken. They see everything, in detail; nothing escapes their sight. Their vision is omnipotent and sharp. And then finally, data analytics are smart. They are the smart thing to be involved with, giving the edge over competitors. These systems are also themselves smart, they blend machine and human intelligence to enhance insight. These things, these dreams, are at the heart of the data imaginary.

There is a powerful logic being propagated here that gives some explanation as to why data analytics spread so rapidly through organisations and through the social world more broadly. This imaginary is an active presence that oils those circulations and shapes their pathways. To understand the role of data in the social world requires us to understand the role of the data analytics industry as both an active presence in the use of data and as a promoter of data-led thinking. In these visions of the power and promises of data analytics we are looking at the cutting-edge of broader processes of data-centred forms of capitalism, competition and calculative logics. The data gaze is rooted in this data imaginary. It is the data imaginary that creates the space, purpose and desire for the analytics and for the data gaze. As with the broader social imaginary, the data gaze is based upon a back and forth between what is imagined and what is practised. Understanding the data imaginary provides the basis for understanding the visions of what the data gaze can achieve and a basis for understanding how the knowledge associated with the data gaze is framed, as well as revealing how its analytical grids are established.

NOTES

1. This article was published in *Network World* on the 13 August 2015 and is available here http://www.networkworld.com/article/2970498/big-data-busi ness-intelligence/13-big-data-and-analytics-companies-to-watch.html Accessed 25 November 2015.
2. This article was published in *Fortune* on the 13 June 2014 and is available here http://fortune.com/2014/06/13/these-big-data-companies-are-ones-to-watch/
3. The materials drawn upon in this sample were all accessed between the 25 November and the 2 December 2015.
4. Appendix, ref 14
5. Appendix, ref 10
6. Appendix, ref 7
7. Appendix, ref 25
8. Appendix, ref 34
9. Take for example this passage: 'The Palantir Metropolis interactive user interface brings abstractions to life in the form of rich visualizations. Tables, scatter plots, and charts interact seamlessly to provide a holistic view of all integrated data of interest. The visualizations update in real-time with the source data, so users always see the most accurate and current information at any given time. Analysts can tweak their logic, test new hypotheses, and present new findings to decision-makers who review the analysis, update their priors, and ask new questions. The enterprise gets smarter, and the cycle continues' (Appendix, ref 25).
10. Appendix, ref 3, 7, 11, 12, 23 & 33
11. Appendix, ref 28
12. Appendix, ref 5
13. Appendix, ref 33
14. Appendix, ref 28
15. Appendix, ref 5, 12 & 22
16 Appendix, ref 16
17. Appendix, ref 27 & 28
18. Appendix, ref 27
19. Appendix, ref 28
20. Appendix, ref 29
21. Appendix, ref 28
22. Appendix, ref 12
23. Appendix, ref 1, 13, 25, 30 & 34
24. Appendix, ref 17, 23, 24, & 33
25. Appendix, ref 17
26. Appendix, ref 33
27. A further example of such claims would include: 'The world runs on data. It's streaming in from every conceivable device, system, process and interaction. While organisations can envision value from their data, harnessing it to inform, guide and accelerate growth remains a struggle' (Appendix, ref 32).
28. Appendix, ref 12

29. Appendix, ref 25
30. Appendix, ref 27
31. Appendix, ref 27
32. Appendix, ref 28
33. Appendix, ref 34
34. Appendix, ref 32
35. Appendix, ref 5
36. Appendix, ref 12
37. Appendix, ref 16
38. Appendix, ref 12; see also ref 13
39. Appendix, ref 14
40. Appendix, ref 8
41. Appendix, ref 10
42. Appendix, ref 11
43. Appendix, ref 31
44. Appendix, ref 13
45. Appendix, ref 23
46. Appendix, ref 26
47. Appendix, ref 34
48. Appendix, ref 8
49. Appendix, ref 18
50. Appendix, ref 1
51. Appendix, ref 3
52. Appendix, ref 8
53. Appendix, ref 17
54. Appendix, ref 8
55. Also in Appendix, ref 10
56. Appendix, ref 8
57. Appendix, ref 10
58. Appendix, ref 24
59. Appendix, ref 5
60. Appendix, ref 19

3

Perpetuating and Deploying a Rationality of Speed: The Temporality of the Data Gaze

In 2016, Hewlett Packard Enterprise ran a full-page advert extolling the virtues of speediness. The advert, illustrated with blurred coloured rectangles set on a black background, opens with the claim that 'Tomorrow belongs to the fast'.[1] It continues, 'winners and losers will quickly be decided by how quickly they can move from what they are now to what they need to become'. The need for speed is repeatedly emphasised across the 136 words of the advert, with the word 'accelerating' used seven times, 'quickly' once, 'fast' once and 'faster' twice. In a short advert the text is dense with speedy ideals. The claim is that 'in every business, IT strategy is now business strategy' and that the result of adapting to this will be: 'Accelerating change. Accelerating growth. Accelerating security.' This move also, it claims, brings: 'Accelerating innovation. Accelerating transformation. Accelerating value.' The advert points continually at a future in which there is a need to act, a kind of urgency to move and a danger to passivity. It closes with the slightly baffling claim: 'accelerating next'. It would seem that the future cannot come quickly enough. This advert captures some of the core ideas that I will explore in this chapter. The idea that to thrive or even survive, the imperative is to be fast and to utilise data. This, as I will show, is a dominant trope. The vision of a faster future is used to promote a move towards data in the present. To win is to be fast, to lose is to be slow.

This chapter seeks to give the data gaze a sense of temporality or urgency. Or, rather, it explores how the data gaze is imbued with a sense of urgency and a need to act quickly. The data gaze has a temporal dimension that is associated with a sense that it is pressing and its processes must be adapted and deployed quickly to manage an accelerating world. Analytics, as I explore, are not temporally neutral – at least not in the way that they are envisioned. Foucault's (2003) account of the gaze in *The Birth of the Clinic* did not pay a great deal of attention to its temporality, at least not beyond the notion of the speed of the glance or the sequential processes that it worked through. Foucault acknowledges that in operating horizontally and vertically the gaze also operates at the level of time, but it is not something he develops at great length. The clinician's gaze is both 'synchronic and diachronic' (Foucault, 2003: 200), he elaborates. This would suggest that it operates both as a form of analysis in the moment and as an ongoing analysis, watching things unfold over time. As Foucault adds, the medical gaze '*analysed a series*' (Foucault, 2003: 200, italics in original). This indicates that it takes sets of observations and watches transformations over time. Such analyses operate at multiple scales and across time – taking snapshots as well as analysing change, mutation and transformation. The 'clinical gaze' analyses in the moment as well as watching for trends, patterns and things evolving. One thing it does not share with the data gaze is quite such the same thirst for prediction. In fact, the clinic space seemed to be based upon giving the medical gaze the time and space that it needed. With the data gaze it is hard to ignore the importance of temporality and speed for understanding how it is presented and how its knowledge is legitimised. Speed is not a peripheral issue but is actually central to understanding the data gaze. Hence it is crucial to incorporate both time and speed.

ANALYTICS IN AN ACCELERATING WORLD

However accurate it might be, it has become something of an accepted notion that we are living in accelerating times. Things are getting quicker. Or so it seems. This notion is particularly notable in the coverage of the transformations associated with data. The escalating promises of the revenue generation that will be achieved through the adoption of analytics are dramatic, as are the imagined pitfalls for those who choose not to (as summarised by the various figures captured by Columbus, 2015). The financial projections of both the analytics industry itself and the projections for those organisations who choose to integrate analytics are predictably mammoth. The faith in the transformative power of data and their attendant analytics is also profound, with common claims like 85% of business leaders believe that big data will lead to significant organisational change and 79% agreeing that 'companies that do not embrace Big Data will lose their competitive position and may even face extinction' (Accenture, in Columbus, 2015). The promises and hazards are powerful in their depicted extremes. To give a little more sense of the scale of this emerging industry of analytics, a 2014 'snapshot' of the total 'worldwide Business Analytics' market put it at $40.3 billion (Vesset et al., 2015). This is an industry that is difficult to define, but this gives a sense of its apparent scale and continued growth.

To give some further detail of the organisations being analysed here, of the business analytics market shares estimated in 2014, the most recent figures that could be located, seven companies had the majority of the market share: of these seven, Oracle (with 17.3%), SAP (with 14.4%) and Teradata (with 3.4%) are included in the sample used for this chapter (see Vesset et al., 2015). Excluding these large seven organisations, the estimate from 2014 shows the remaining 37.4% of the market to be covered by all other providers. This then is not a complete vision of the market, plus it focuses on software providers as opposed to all analytics services, but it gives a sense of the size and make-up of this emergent industry. It also gives a sense of the sample I am working with here, which includes analytics providers of different sizes and with varying market shares.

In this particular chapter I will focus specifically upon how data are seen to provide opportunities for rapid analytics and for forms of real-time knowledge. I am concerned here with understanding how the data analytics industry attempts to perpetuate a wider perception of cultural and organisational acceleration whilst also then presenting data analytics as a potential solution to the need to keep up. This is not an argument about the material speed-up of analytics, instead it explores how the perception of speed-up is used to promote the expansion of analytic processes. The accounts of data analytics that this industry provides, which of course are geared towards expanding its market and rolling out data-led processes, are premised upon a sort of accelerated knowledge that enables organisations to be increasingly responsive, nimble and reactive to market pressures. Acting as data intermediaries, by providing products and services for those desiring data analytics solutions, this emergent analytics industry has achieved increasing influence in recent years. This influence is associated with both the analytics that they provide and also with the way in which they theorise, represent and project power onto data. The analytics industry is tapping into a wider rationality, in which speed and agility are seen to be crucial.

Building upon the previous chapter, this chapter is used to extend one particularly prominent aspect of the data imaginary: speed. It continues to work with the sample of 34 data analytics providers (see Appendix) in order to explore the rhetorical framing of the speediness of the data analytic solutions that they offer.[2] The wider general perceptions of cultural speed-up frame understandings of organisational life; it is against this backdrop that data analytics are presented as a potential solution to the need to speed up and to keep up with the competition. As a result, it is argued that notions of speedy analytics are central to the spread and intensification of data-led decision making, governance and ordering processes. The promises of real-time knowing are one means by which organisational speed and agility are seen to be achievable; the result is the pushing back of the limits of what has been referred to as 'datafication' (van Dijck, 2014) and an increase in the field of vision of the data gaze.

This chapter is concerned with the power of the data analytics industry and the powerful ways in which this industry presents and projects properties and promises onto data and data analytics. It suggests that this industry taps into, cultivates and then attempts to deploy the wider rationality of *a need for speed*.

Within a broader data imaginary – in which promises, ideals and values are projected onto data – this chapter focuses upon the visions of speed that are promoted or conjured by this data analytics industry. The central argument I make is that visions of speediness and the promises of real-time knowing are central to the spread and intensification of data-led processes throughout the social world. Which is to say that by emphasising the need to turn to data analytics as a means to keep up with an accelerating world of ever speedier and more efficient competitors, the data analytics industry is generating a vision of data that has consequences for wider social and organisational structures and ordering. To understand the spread of data and data analytics into the practices and routines of everyday life – as they come to lace with evaluation and judgement – we need not just to look at the practices of data analytics but also to look at how those analytics are imagined into existence (which we might see as fitting with the programme of work around the cultural dynamics of data mining suggested by Andrejevic et al., 2015). This chapter shows how understandings of data and data analytics are actively being produced, but it also provides an explorative illustration of the construction of notions of cultural and social speed-up. Here mobilities of data are presented as being so rapid that they bring knowledge about the world into real-time thus closing the gap, it is suggested, between data and knowledge or between data and decisive action.

The chapter begins by focusing upon wider notions of cultural speed-up. This provides some sense of the conditions in which these tropes of speedy analytics are being forged. This also gives us the background for exploring the growing sense of the need to speed up, to which data analytics are then presented as *the* solution. I then focus upon some of the ways in which the speed of data analytics is presented by the data analytics industry, especially as it attempts to play off this backdrop of a perception of a speedier world. That is to say that it explores what Doughty and Murray (2016) have referred to as 'institutional discourses of mobility' as they relate to data. In unpicking these framings of speedy data analytics, the chapter looks at the breaking of the limits of 'datafication' (van Dijck, 2014) and then explores the scale of these speedy analytics, the notions of data-led keep-up and the powerful promises of real-time knowing. Together these reveal the way in which narratives of speed are utilised to push back the data frontiers and expand the scope, coverage and intensity of data-led processes.

CULTURES OF SPEED: AN ACCELERATING WORLD?

What this has suggested so far is that the 'social life of methods' (see for example Savage, 2013) is not just about the circulation of technique, it is also about the circulation of the imaginary that surrounds both methods and data. Indeed, Turow et al. (2015) have argued that there is a 'social imaginary' around the practice of data mining that makes its associated practices feel like a 'natural part of life'. The practices of consumers are reconfigured by the reshaping of the social imaginary – data mining here then is a product of this imaginary as well as the technical assemblage (see Turow et al., 2015: 465–7). In this chapter, though, I am thinking more directly about the reshaping of the social imaginary with regard to the reconfiguration of organisational practices. Before we begin to explore the details of the imaginary that is provided by the data analytics industry, it is worth pausing to reflect on the broader context in which these framings occur.

When it comes to the mobilities that constitute the social world, a key notion is that we are living in times of speed-up or acceleration. However materially accurate this may be, there is a dominant perception that things are getting quicker. The 2008 financial crisis, the ripples of which are still being felt in many different national contexts, led to some reinvigorated debates on the relative merits or dangers of acceleration in terms of empowerment and disempowerment (Gardiner, 2017). This has filtered down to discussions of how an accelerated world impacts upon individuals and how either speeding up or slowing down might address these social issues – with the possibilities of attempts to 'slow down modernity' becoming a source of debate along with the politics of the solutions tied up within these notions (Vostal, 2017). In an agenda-setting piece, Hartmut Rosa (2003: 4) made the claim that 'we cannot adequately understand the nature and character of modernity and the logic of its structural and cultural development unless we add the temporal perspective to our analysis'. This is not a contentious point in itself, it is the reason for this focus that is important in Rosa's work. Rosa places 'social acceleration' at the centre of the analysis. Rosa explores the acceleration of technology, social change and the pace of life as they are driven by what he describes as economic, cultural and social 'motors'. One key conclusion drawn by Rosa (2003: 27) is that 'acceleration is an irreducible and constitutive trait of modernization'. This is not a universal account of acceleration, but there is, he argues, a 'great many social phenomena to which the concept of acceleration can properly be applied' (Rosa, 2003: 5). This chapter will not explore the actual temporality of things, nor will it draw conclusions on whether social life is actually accelerating, but it will look at the importance of how those temporalities are imagined and projected onto social structures and processes. Clearly then, speed and acceleration are on the agenda both in terms of the analysis of the current state of things and how these might be experienced and shaped in the future.

Around 15 years ago Scott Lash (2002: 137–9) reflected on what it means to live in such an 'age of speed'. This is an age in which, he contends, we have little space for critical reflection outside of the flow of information to which we are exposed. Similarly Gane (2006: 20), around a decade ago, claimed that 'it is hard to think of an aspect of human existence that has yet to be touched by the fast technologies of the new media age'. To pick an example of this type of perception of ubiquitous acceleration, we can turn to Hand et al.'s (2005) discussion of the notions of speed, temporality and immediacy associated with developments in domestic showering technologies. This illustrates the embedding of narratives of speed into all sorts of technological shifts. Thinking across scales, Sassen (2006: 386) discusses the need to appreciate the variable temporalities that occur, especially as they range between bodily experiences through to global processes. Sassen's suggestion is to focus on 'analytical borderlands' in which these varying temporalities come to intersect. In short, it would seem that Sassen is arguing for focused explorations of cases of acceleration that are sensitised to the uneven nature of that acceleration. Despite some questions being raised about the nature of this acceleration, Gane (2006: 21) notes that there 'is broad agreement that new media technologies are transforming lived experience … , not least because they are introducing new, ever-faster practices of communication, which in turn are altering the basis of social interaction'. It would seem that over the last 20 years there has been some agreement that social life has been accelerating, especially in association with the integration of new media forms (see also Virilio, 1991: 59, 95). This perceived acceleration appears to occur on a range of scales, from global processes to organisational and individual lives. As Tomlinson (2007: 1) has put it in his book on cultural speed-up, 'acceleration rather than deceleration has been the constant leitmotiv of cultural modernity'. Tomlinson's observation is that we have a cultural tendency towards the perception that acceleration is desirable. Calls for slowness are relatively marginal when contrasted with the broader push towards speed. However, there have been a number of slow culture type movements since the writing of Tomlinson's book – such as slow food, the slow academy and the like – that hint at a little more resistance in recent years and an increasingly potent 'critique of accelerationism' (Gardiner, 2017).

Following on from his earlier work, Lash has argued that this speed-up has factored in the emergence of a kind of 'intensive culture' (Lash, 2010). We live, Lash claims (2010: 3), 'in a culture that is at the same time extensive and intensive'. The core idea here is that capitalism both spreads outwards whilst, simultaneously, increasing its intensity within our everyday lives. Networks for Lash increase in both reach and density. Here, according to Lash, the 'pace' and 'volume' of experience increase, as do our interactions and transactions. Capitalism's forces are not seen to be watered down, diluted or distributed as they spread, instead, for Lash, they reach outwards whilst increasing their intensity. Capitalism is seen to expand outwards whilst also increasingly being focused inwards, on individual lives. From this perspective we would need to look across organisational structures to understand how broader shifts impinge on the feeling of acceleration for individual experience. In this formulation the speeding up of culture is associated with the stretch and increasing intensity of our experiences of capitalism, on a global and individual scale. This is close to an application of what Paul Virilio famously referred to as 'dromology'. Dromology, as Virilio puts it, refers to 'the importance of speed in history, and thus of acceleration' (Virilio, in Armitage, 2001: 16). Dromology, for Virilio, as he discusses in an interview with John Armitage (2001: 26), is concerned with understanding the role of speed and acceleration in wealth and power distributions. Virilio's point is that transport and information have accelerated what he calls the 'quest for the attainment of real time' (Virilio, in Armitage, 2001: 27). This quest is something to which we will return; the point here is that these accelerations of culture are a product of both the spreading *and* intensification of capitalist processes.

Indeed, these types of assertions amongst other observations have led Judy Wajcman (2015: 1) to conclude that 'there is a widespread perception that life these days is faster than it used to be'. What is crucial here is the idea that complexities around temporality and the rate at which lives are actually lived are often hidden behind such a reductive perception. As Wajcman (2015: 5–6) puts it, 'there are both different senses of feeling pressed for time and a range of mechanisms that trigger those feelings'. Which, Wajcman (2015: 9–10) indicates, then draw us towards the need for a careful unpicking of the dynamics of these feelings of time pressure, particularly as they link to the liberating and contrasting powers of new technologies. The key point here is that although it might appear that life is accelerating, this assertion may obscure the realities of temporal experience. One key issue is that, as Wajcman (2015: 6) points out, 'talk about life accelerating only makes sense against an implied backdrop of a slower past'. The issue is with the ability or inability to measure and compare acceleration at the level of the social, the cultural or the individual. It is, of course, almost impossible to imagine being able to verify such claims to social acceleration given these observations – it would require both a sense of the speed of life at some point in the past and a way of measuring the pace of life today. Given the complexity that Wajcman is intimating here, how could we possibly even begin to measure how time pressures are felt today, let alone in the past? What is important here is the generally held perception that life is getting quicker and that time pressures are more acute. The empirical realities of the pace of life are not of concern here. It would seem that the importance of the feeling or notion of acceleration is what is particularly powerful. This is the perception that we will later see the data analytics industry perpetuating and then using to carve out a niche.

The ultimate destination of this speed-up is what Tomlinson calls 'the condition of immediacy' (Tomlinson, 2007: 72). This is where acceleration reaches the point at which everything is experienced instantly. As Tomlinson explains, 'this is to think of immediacy particularly in its temporal mode: of closing the gap in *time* or more precisely, of abolishing *waiting*' (Tomlinson, 2007: 92, italics in the original). This is found in the closing of the gap between production and consumption, the tightening of the gap between event and realisation, a narrowing of feedback loops. We can clarify this by turning to Mark Andrejevic's (2013) concept of 'immediation'. Andrejevic (2013: 146) argues that this type of notion of a closing of the gap in production and consumption is typical of a variety of attempts to construct 'a fantasy of "immediation" that takes the shape of either direct access to knowledge in the real (neuromarketing, body language analysis) or by sidestepping the need for comprehension altogether (predictive analytics, decision markets, sentiment analysis)'. The idea here is that representation can be bypassed, or at least the impression is given that it can be bypassed, in favour of more instant or direct forms of knowledge. These, for Andrejevic, are fantasies or myths about the accessibility and form that knowledge can take with the rise of big data and what he calls the 'infoglut'. It is a story that will resonate in the descriptions I provide in the following pages.

This closing of *the gap* or 'immediation' is something we will revisit, especially as we explore the perception of the closing of the gap in the production of real-time knowledge about the social world. For the moment though we can see how a cultural shift in speediness, towards notions of unrelenting acceleration, creates conditions in which temporal gaps are seen to be reduced and in which the desire to avoid waiting becomes significant in the conduct of everyday life. The pressure then is upon people to manage and respond to this immediacy and to find their way around the need for flexibility and reactivity. This imperative for speed resonates across a range of scales. Tomlinson (2007: 159) closes by claiming that the 'virtue to be found in speed is … to apply effort to become nimble and graceful life-performers'. We will see how the data analytics industry plays to such an apparent virtue, along with the appeal to be responsive and agile performers. It is in such values that we find the types of imperatives to acceleration are cultivated by the data analytics industry. The sense here is that agility in response to acceleration is a primary virtue, and that there is a need to find ways to achieve such nimbleness. If we regard these as cultivated values rather than concrete social facts, then we can begin to unpick the way in which they are cultivated, maintained and then utilised to shape change or to provoke behaviours. For the purposes of this chapter it matters not so much if cultural speed-up is an empirical reality, it is the perception of speed-up that really matters here. It is the *feeling of acceleration* that is being cultivated to which we might see the data analytics industry both contributing and responding. This chapter aims at unpicking these visions and promises of speed associated with data analytics, and how these are presented as a response to the notions of cultural and social speed-up.

SPEEDING PAST THE LIMITS OF DATAFICATION

Data analytics are dominated by notions of speed. As was outlined in the previous chapter, there are a number of themes within the data imaginary, but speediness, immediacy and the promises of real-time knowing are particularly prominent. These are products and solutions accompanied by claims such as: 'The fastest easiest way to understand your data'[3], or 'Fast analytics for everyone'[4], or 'Fast-cycle Business-ready insights on more data'[5] and 'We provide the world's fastest, easiest, and most secure data platform'[6]. Speed dominates. There is a sense here of a profound need for acceleration. Effective and productive data analytics are seen to be fast data analytics. Good analytics are those that are seen to produce instant results. These various formulations are clearly aimed at cultivating the image that data analytics are the means by which organisational practice and decision making can accelerate. Of course, a key aspect of the work being done by the marketing rhetoric of data analytics is the expansion of the market in which they operate. They want more organisations to integrate data analytics within their structures of governance. That is to say, the aim of this rhetoric is to expand the scope and intensity of data-led processes. This is about breaking through the boundaries of datafication by enabling 'data collection without limits' (Andrejevic, 2013: 36). The aim is to push back what might be thought of as the data frontiers. As discussed in Chapter 2, these are the borders that data processes have not yet reached or beyond which they are yet to be fully integrated. The emphasis on the speed of data analytics is designed to break through such boundaries or limits. We find then that notions of speed are imported to give the sense that such boundaries can be broken through or smashed, thus enabling new organisational possibilities. The emphasis is upon data mobilities and the promises of real-time knowing. Speediness is the key promise that is made about the value of analytics, and is thus particularly active in attempts to make data frontiers more porous. Data analytics are presented as being able to rapidly give you what you need to know. Strategic thinking and self-training individuals are indicated as being the prerequisites to organisational success. As such, promises of speedy analytics are the crux for the breaking of the limits of datafication and the spread of analytic, calculative and data-led processes throughout the social world.

This can be seen in the way that this industry presents data analytics as a proxy for organisational acceleration and the speeding past or breaking through of boundaries and limits. Speedy knowledge is presented as being disruptive to established boundaries. As it is put in one instance:

> Break the speed limit at your desk. Ready. Set. Done. Platfora's in-memory query engine and massive parallel processing architecture let you crunch petabytes of data at the speed of thought – your thoughts, that is.[7]

The image here is of the relatively passive user, sat at their desk, being able to suddenly achieve accelerated practices and decision making through the analytic software. The organisation operates, in this vision, at the speed of thought. The image is of data analytics allowing organisational speed-up to become possible, with the only constraint being the speed of thought of the individual.

The limits of the speed of action, it is suggested, come from the human actor rather than the analytic processes. As machine agency meshes with human agency the decision making occurs at the speed of thought of the human actor, or so the message goes. The image then is of rapid knowledge production that operates more quickly than human thought. The depiction of the speed of thought of the analytic device suggests that it is always ready to produce ongoing knowledge that facilitates the acceleration of action. The only limit, it is suggested, being the speed at which the human actor can think and respond to the revelations and insights being produced. In other words, the above passage suggests that the analytics can enable organisations to move at a speed that reflects their ability to react to the insights produced. The videos that are frequently found to support these types of claims present an audio-visual image of the fracturing of boundaries and the speediness of analytics, with quick cuts and rapidly forming graphs, charts and other visualisations appearing in a disembodied vision of active and rapid machine-based knowledge formation. The result is the envisioning of the breaking of both the limits of action and the limits of datafication at the same time – with new possibilities for both. This is a quicker whilst more data-intensive vision of organisations in which data analytics are presented as the means to remove constraints.

It is the volume and quantity of the data that is said to be the means for breaking such boundaries. As the above would suggest, this apparent speediness is often linked to a desire for agility – with the size of the data being presented as providing little obstacle to the speediness of the analytics. These data are said to be big yet this bulk does not weigh down these imagined organisational structures, the analytics remain fast. This is a combination, we are told, of 'SCALE, SPEED, AGILITY'[8]. The idea, it would seem, is that this is speed at scale. The size of the data is not cumbersome but is a facilitator of responsiveness. As is suggested in this passage:

> Speed at scale. Trillion rows in 3 seconds, billions in less. Interana provides access to 100% of the raw event data with the speed to easily ask series of questions in seconds, without the consequence of being wrong. Interana's scale keeps the richness of data by not requiring aggregations or summarizations often used to shrink it into other solutions.[9]

As well as drawing upon notions of 'raw' data, which we have seen questioned (see Gitelman, 2013), here we see a quantification of scale is used to emphasise the point that this is, as it is put, speed at scale. Thinking quickly, it is claimed, can occur without the increased risk of mistakes that usually comes with rapid responses. Here, agility is attached to the use of large-scale analytics. Despite the scope of the data, these analytics are depicted as enabling rapid inference without hesitation. This works against the probably common sense notion that increases in data are likely to slow down analytical insights. Again, this vision emphasises the idea that these analytics are comprehensive whilst also being quick. The result, it is suggested, is that organisations can use that scale and speed to be informed and nimble in their activities. Big data, despite their apparently colossal volume, are able to facilitate agility. At least that is the message that appears to be conveyed here. Again, we see how notions of competitiveness and the need to keep up seep through in the depictions of the power of these analytics.

KEEPING UP WITH AN ACCELERATING WORLD OF DATA: THE ENVISIONING OF SPEEDIER PRACTICE

The implicit diktat is that there is a need to accelerate practice so as to keep up with the accelerating world. The analytics industry cultivates and nurtures the risk of being left behind if you choose to take the slow route and not adopt the speediness of these analytics. As might be expected, older and more established processes are imported as points of juxtaposition that illustrate the possibilities for the acceleration. For example, the claim is made that: 'Traditional data infrastructure procurement and deployment takes months and is too costly to support fast-growing data volumes'[10]. The costliness of such a slow pace is a central part of the message here, and the key driver for the need to speed up. These are presented as being 'faster business outcomes at a fraction of the cost'[11]. Slowness, it would seem, is equated with wastefulness. The slowness of non-data informed practices is contrasted to the lightning speed of data analytics. Analytics are presented as solutions to slowness, with the suggestion that 'there's a way around this with built-in intelligent data inferencing, and automated data blending and harmonization solutions that speed and ease this otherwise tedious process'[12]. This is an account in which slow organisational structures can be circumvented, reconfigured or usurped by the knowledge provided through these data analytics.

Narratives of waste are coupled with risks of inefficiency. The sense is that not integrating data analytics will bring slowness, which in turn will bring on either sudden catastrophe or slow demise. Established practices become moribund in an age of data, it is suggested. This is the context in which, we are warned, others will take advantage of the opportunities if you do not – as is suggested by the claim that, 'the ability to have fast, interactive, visual insights into business performance can mean the difference between success and failure'[13]. The promises of success come with being fast, whilst failure is attached to slowness. Again, we see the desirability of the hyper-competitive, strategic and knowledge-based organisation to be an implicit presence in these accounts. This is encapsulated in the notions of waste and wastefulness that take centre stage and promote an urgency for rapid efficiency:

> Today, the biggest challenge in any analytical exercise is simply getting the data you need ready. Bringing together multiple data sets from different sources, looking for duplicate data or blank fields, fixing misspellings, splitting or reshaping columns, adding additional data to provide more context. As quickly as data is being made available, and with all of the amazing Business Intelligence tools at your fingertips, every minute wasted on data preparation is a minute you are not asking questions and making decisions.[14]

We are returned in the above passage to the combination of speed and scale, but this time the scale comes from the intersectional use of multiple sources of data. The analytics here are informed by a comprehensive but instant grasp of *all* of the available data. This is required, the above suggests, to avoid the loss of time. Here time becomes the thing that is wasted where there is an absence of data analytics. The message is that the time spent trying to do things can be saved. With this image of data analytics, wasted preparation time is redeployed to do more thinking, to ask more questions and then to be more strategic. The mere presence of the data, in the above case, exposes waste and implies the need to access knowledge more quickly to inform questions and decision making. The data gaze is laced with a sense of urgency.

These accounts emphasise internal organisational speed-up and the possibilities that are associated with speedy analytics, but we also find visions of the acceleration of the external world. Which in turn then cultivates the need to speed up. It is not just about the wastefulness of being slow, it is that the world is an accelerating data-led place and acceleration is necessary in order to just keep up, never mind get ahead. As is suggested by this excerpt:

> In this hyper-connected world, with data volumes constantly increasing, analytics solutions from SAP can help you to simplify, innovate, and accelerate. Make your life easier by analysing, predicting, and running your business in real time. Discover and execute on innovations that create value for your organisation. And achieve rapid insight into action across your organisation, closing the gap between transactions, data preparation, analysis, and action – all with analytics.[15]

You can both, it suggests, make life easier whilst also responding to the demands of this hyper-connected world. The software packages and analytics solutions become the means by which it is possible to accelerate to the speed of this accelerating world. The image then is of a world of data that is getting quicker, the only way to respond is to join in and engage with the possibilities that those data bring. The only way to keep up with an accelerating world and marketplace is to accelerate through the deployment of data analytics. The above passage also contains the notion of 'closing the gap', to which we can now turn.

SO FAST, IT IS INSTANT: THE PROMISES OF REAL-TIME KNOWING

Earlier we saw Paul Virilio's suggestion that there is a 'quest for real time' in the pursuit of speedier information, a quest that is tempered somewhat with Andrejevic's (2013) point about the fantasy of 'immediation'. It would seem, however, that this quest still pertains in the framing of data analytics.

The message in this regard is that these data analytics are so fast, they are instant. The move is from post-hoc analytics, to analytics that occur in the moment. These analytics are said to reveal the world as it unfolds, without delay. To refer back again to the earlier discussions, the depiction of data analytics is that there is no 'gap'. The result of closing the gap between data and insight is that the analytics are then operating, it is suggested, in real-time. The depiction is that they are 'immediated' (Andrejevic, 2013) and produce direct forms of knowledge that *access the real in real-time*. The notion of 'real-time' permeates the industry's messages and is a commonly evoked term aimed at producing a sense of instantaneity and speed of both insight and subsequent action. The promises of real-time knowing are based around the possibility of reacting quickly, gaining an edge, winning the competition and even anticipating future events.

Visions of an immediated real-time abound. Here is one typical example of the deployment of this frequently used phrase: 'DataTorrent empowers today's enterprises to experience the full potential – and business impact – of big data, by enabling them to process, analyze, make decisions and take action on data in real-time'[16]. Operating in real-time here is part of enabling the full potential of the data – projecting powerful promises of acceleration upon them. This is the promise that is being made. Using data quickly gets at hidden value. As this particular organisation then emphasises, despite moving rapidly this is seen to be a form of decision making 'with no risks, constraints, management overhead or performance degradation'[17]. Despite operating in real-time, the lack of time for reflection is presented as holding no risk. So it makes it possible to be reactionary without the usual problems that we might associate with decision making without reflection. The emphasis is upon the maintenance of accuracy whilst operating at a real-time speed of analysis. As it is put in another instance, 'the visualizations update in real-time with the source data, so users always see the most accurate and current information at any given time'[18]. Accurate and current – these are depicted as forms of knowledge that are trustworthy despite their quick reactions.

This thinking at speed is not only seen to increase accuracy, as is fitting with the broader data imaginary the promises of real-time knowing are also portrayed as being smart and intelligent. These are presented as active learning systems that enable quick analytical insights. As one organisation put it, 'Our software allows you to not only collect your customers' data, but also act on it intelligently in real-time'[19]. The narratives of smartness that permeate many such technologies are present here – mixing the data imaginary's properties of speed and smartness. In this case the software is both presented as intelligent itself whilst also facilitating intelligent decision making in human actors – which is part of a broader set of understandings of the way that algorithms interact with human cognition (see Williamson, 2017). The emphasis of the data imaginary is upon the speed and accuracy of the gaze and the potential of the instantaneous glance.

As the above suggests, the claims are about the analytics' ability to facilitate quick and well-informed decisions. As one provider adds:

> Real-Time Decisioning. The days of segmentation and batch predictions sufficing for your customers are behind us. Our platform makes every decision in real-time, using everything there is to know about a customer up until the very last moment.[20]

Here a comparison with a more sedentary past is used to provide an image of a slower world, whereas the quick analytics, in counterdistinction, enable the decision making to occur in real-time. Thus, it is imagined, closing the gap between data capture and action. The notion of 'the last moment' is used in the above passage to suggest that this is an ongoing production in which the most recent data feed immediately into visualised outcomes and insights – it also suggests a temporal limit. There is an unceasing rhythm to the analytics, with decisions constantly informed by the data gathered in that very moment. Despite closing the gap and producing knowledge in the moment, these are also constantly switched-on systems that produce ongoing insights – they are described as 'real-time, continuous, comprehensive'[21]. The data gaze is thus charged with an unrelenting urgency. The knowledge associated with the data gaze takes on such properties.

The above illustrates the notions of accuracy and intelligence that become part of the promises of real-time knowing cultivated by the data analytics industry. Beyond this we see a predictive or prophetic element to these promises – again the presence of speed combines with the other features of the wider data imaginary. The impression is that acting in real-time also enables decision making that is anticipatory of future outcomes. This is illustrated by claims such as 'Neokami's algorithmic engine is able to accurately (up to 98%) partition the customer base regardless of the dimensional complexity of the customer behavior and red flags high-risk churners before churning in real-time so that you can take action before it's too late'[22]. Again we are reminded, in this version of what Taina Bucher (2017) has called the 'algorithmic imaginary', of the sense of burgeoning catastrophe that concerns the need to take action before it is 'too late' – with data analytics ensuring the quick action needed for survival. Beyond this though there is the idea that by operating in real-time it is possible to take action, potentially holding on to customers before they decide to move or protecting revenue streams before loss. The promise of real-time knowing in this case is one of anticipation and the ability to cultivate a kind of ramped-up proactivity – acting before people make choices that might be to the detriment of the organisation.

Finally, the promises of real-time knowing come wrapped in claims to the accessibility of the knowledge being produced by these systems. These solutions, it is envisioned, afford accessible speediness. There are, we are told, 'integrated and controllable dashboards ... made for the marketer, allowing them to filter, drill down and summarize data in meaningful ways that clarify actions in real time'[23]. And elsewhere that a particular package:

> ... speeds up big data payoff with Hadoop, through data-driven apps you create with drag-and-drop ease, eliminating barriers to big data utilization. You get fast, direct transparent visualization and analysis across all your big data.[24]

The term 'drag-and-drop ease', a phrase that is likely to denote a familiar technique, is used to suggest the accessibility and intuitiveness of the software and the minimal technical skill required to operate it quickly. This is a form of analytical insight, we are told, from which meaning can be easily and quickly derived by any user. The data can be explored in ways that are seen to be intuitive and accessible, meaning that the speed at which they can be used is also instant. As it is put in one case, these packages: 'Enable behavioral analytics on event data with a fast, visual, and intuitive solution accessible to all'[25]. There is no delay, it is opined, in extracting meaning because of the ease with which that real-time knowledge about events can be accessed. The speediness is associated with *a reduced need for the interpretation* of these instant insights. Here we see again how those fantasies of immediation, to which Andrejevic (2013: 77) refers, can be found in these visions of direct and instant knowledge that seems to bypass mediation – somehow gaining, as Andrejevic (2013: 112) pointed out, direct access to the real. It is suggested that such a package 'gives everyone the power to explore, analyze, and question your big data in real time'[26] or that you can use them to 'Make your life easier by analysing, predicting, and running your business in real time'[27]. Everyone then, it would seem, has an easier and more instant grasp of the real-time world with the integration of data analytics. This makes everyone a quick and nimble data analyst, turning the user into the expert, an expert with access to all types of data-informed insights. Immediation reaches its peak where software transforms us into our own data analysts. This is to 'combine'[28] forms of data in a 'holistic approach'[29] to 'support predictive analytics, real-time dashboards, master data management and more'[30]. Nothing, it would seem, can escape the instant analytic glance. These real-time dashboards are presented as being the means by which data are instantly accessible for ongoing analysis. Such promises of real-time knowing are a central part of the framing of data analytics, particularly in relation to the promotion of notions of accuracy, intelligence, anticipation and accessibility. These are the promises of *real-time knowing* projected onto the affordances of data analytics.

CONCLUSION

The data gaze has a temporality, that temporality is the product of its underlying politics and commercial dynamics. We have only touched the surface of the dominant tropes of speed and speediness that are embedded in the depiction of the power and promises of data analytics. Yet, despite only beginning to unravel these narratives, the above illustrates how data analytics are presented as an antidote or solution to the problem of keeping up with an apparently accelerating world. The data analytics industry aims to both perpetuate and deploy the sense of social and cultural acceleration, enabling it to present data analytics as affording options for keeping up. It would also seem that an accelerated world means accelerated competition, at least that is how it is presented. These are market-based forms of competition that are injected with the vitalising hype of big data and data analytics. Cultivating such an image of accelerating social worlds and speeding competition is a central part of how data-led processes are spreading through organisational, social and everyday life. We saw earlier in this chapter how this sense of acceleration operates on a range of scales. Data analytics are presented as the mechanism by which organisations can stay in the competitive game by turning to data. Andrejevic's use of the concept of 'immediation' is valuable in seeing how these analytics are conveyed as offering an accelerated and accessible form of real-time knowledge. This particular vision of the spreading of the 'model of the market' (Brown, 2015) is perceived as a space of acceleration where the slow are left behind and where datafication is the only rational option.

The way that these speedy analytics are imagined – the data imaginary – becomes a part of how they are understood, adopted and integrated into organisational and everyday life. As with the previous chapter, I have focused on the textual accounts of the data but the accompanying videos used by these providers emphasise the same points: they present quick moving images set to rhythmic music beats, they cut between changing visualisations, with rapidly appearing and disappearing visuals, graphs and images sliding on and off the screen. The audio and visual impressions match those of the text and emphasise speed and a constantly pulsing rhythm, often reflected in the soundtrack.

It is not that these visions are necessarily a reality for how those data analytics ultimately play out, but they nonetheless perform a significant role in getting organisations to buy into datafication. Notions of speed are crucial in pushing back these limits and in expanding the reach of social ordering through data. This suggests that visions of rapid and instant ways of knowing are an important if not central part of the seductive allure of datafication and the expansion of data-led or data-informed processes. Narratives of speediness facilitate the spread of data-informed social ordering and expand the limits of datafication – breaking through the barriers. Quick analytics are seen to equate to progressive and forward-looking organisational structures. The quicker the better, that is the common reasoning. The more data informed the smarter we are thought to be. It has been argued that the model of the market is spreading into social spaces in which it was previously absent (see Brown, 2015; Dean, 2009: 51; Gane, 2012: 632; Peck, 2010: 24). Visions of speedy analytics may be one active presence in the roll-out of such models. The discursive projection of mobilities is not something that is somehow detached from the rise of data, rather it is central to how those data are understood and treated. In this regard, speediness is a key part of the promises being made about data analytics. The objective is to make organisations of different types *feel the need for speed*.

The promise is that competitive positioning and future proofing is to be achieved through the speed of the analytics being used. Speedy analytics are the means or mechanisms by which this type of competition-savvy organisation is said to be reachable. If the ethos or aim is to draw upon knowledge and an understanding of the game (Davies, 2014: 30), then the desirable nimble organisation of today, it would seem, is based on an expertise and knowledge that draws upon real-time analytics. The nature of the knowledge base that is to be drawn upon and the imaginary that surrounds it are changing the perception of the market, of competition and of what it is to be competitive. This is the discursive realisation of what John Tomlinson (2007) previously called the 'condition of immediacy'. We see that there is an impulse to be immediate and to respond to the broader conditions of instantaneity. The visions of speedy analytics and the need to keep up with an accelerating world are propagated by the data analytics industry as they seek the expansion and intensification of data-informed processes. What I have described here is a part of the building and deployment of a rationality of speed. A rationality in which we are made to feel our slowness and where we are led to believe that we need to speed up and be more agile. The data analytics industry may not be the only source of such a prevalent logic, but they appear to be keen to both tap into its presence and to use it as an opportunity to unveil data as the means by which we might answer such pressures to accelerate.

As this shows, the data gaze is impressed with a sense of urgency. The data gaze may be sequential in a similar way to Foucault's clinical gaze, yet its un-anchoring from the fixed analytical space allows it to deploy an ever more instantaneous glance. Constant and ongoing vigilance is a driver and aim of this knowledge. It is not a gaze that is contained in the time and space of the clinical setting, the data gaze is envisioned to work with haste and to be able to do this without hesitation. This vision of the data gaze is reliant, this suggests, upon an infrastructure that is itself immaterial and instant in its presentation of the data and in affording analytics (see Chapter 4).

Foucault described the rapid 'glance' deployed in the clinical setting. The glance, Foucault says, is to practise a kind of targeted gaze. Foucault (2003: 149) explains that the 'glance, on the other hand, does not scan a field: it strikes at one point, which is central or decisive; the gaze is endlessly modulated, the glance goes straight to its object'. He also adds that 'the glance chooses a line that instantly distinguishes the essential' (Foucault, 2003: 149). The gaze, this suggests, is discerning: it is able to quickly identify and single out what matters (this is something we will explore again when we look at the glance of the data analyst in Chapter 5). Siisiäinen's (2013: 27) reading of this point is that this is about the 'immediacy' of an instantaneous glance combined with the possibility of seeing across the 'totality'. The gaze scopes and the glance is targeted. The glance is aimed at a point of analysis and is quick in isolating the crucial or essential features and properties for categorisation and comparison. The glance being made is decisive and direct, homing in on its object and drawing out the required information to populate the analytical grid. The type of rapid 'glance' discussed by Foucault is taken to much greater extremes here: with the glance being instantaneous and in constant motion, always seeking the next targeted insight as the data keep rolling in. The pursuit of the data gaze includes the pursuit of an ever more rapid and targeted glance. Unlike the inspection of the features of the body, the data keep on accumulating and changing, which changes the expectations placed upon the gaze and the knowledge it pursues. Not only does the data gaze have a temporal dimension, it is charged with the politics of a wider notion of cultural change and with ideals about what is needed to manage that change. The temporality of the data gaze is driven by wider notions of time, speed and acceleration. This chapter illustrates the sense that a need for speed is a crucial part of how data generate value, with analytics operating to facilitate keep-up. These visions create an expectation that the infrastructure will allow the data gaze to be deployed ever more quickly and directly. It is to this infrastructure that we now turn.

NOTES

1. This was a full-page advert published in the national politics and culture weekly magazine *The New Statesman.*
2. Based upon this sample of materials from these 34 data analytics companies (see Appendix), this chapter focuses very specifically upon the references made to speed, speediness, rapidity and any other temporal or spatial references to the mobility and pace of the data analytics solutions presented. As discussed in the previous chapter, it was clear that speed and speediness were dominant themes. The initial read through of the materials produced this initial insight and the sample materials were captured in a document which was searched for key words relating to speed. This included speed itself, as well as a range of associated words, such as rapid, slow, quick, fast, immediate, until a second document was created using these references to speed; this second document then became the basis for the following analysis.
3. Appendix, ref 3
4. Appendix, ref 15
5. Appendix, ref 17
6. Appendix, ref 22
7. Appendix, ref 28
8. Appendix, ref 25
9. Appendix, ref 7

10. Appendix, ref 2
11. Appendix, ref 2
12. Appendix, ref 17
13. Appendix, ref 33
14. Appendix, ref 11
15. Appendix, ref 34
16. Appendix, ref 4
17. Appendix, ref 4
18. Appendix, ref 25
19. Appendix, ref 19
20. Appendix, ref 19
21. Appendix, ref 16
22. Appendix, ref 8
23. Appendix, ref 13
24. Appendix, ref 1
25. Appendix, ref 7
26. Appendix, ref 28
27. Appendix, ref 34
28. Appendix, ref 16
29. Appendix, ref 13
30. Appendix, ref 31

The Infrastructural Dimensions of the Data Gaze: The Analytical Spaces of the Codified Clinic

It was an unexpectedly dramatic and somewhat grandiose opening for a software convention. More like something from a TV talent show or an arena rock show. Yet the stage was set in a way that reflected the ambition of the characters behind it – perhaps more so than the understated stage presence of the lead protagonist. Following an elaborate laser-light show, accompanied by a booming techno soundtrack, the DataWorks Summit 2017 opened with a keynote from the chief executive officer of Hortonworks, Rob Bearden. Bearden's keynote address commenced by focusing upon the shared accomplishments of recent times and the pivotal role of *the community* in crucial project developments. Later in the talk he reflected on what he saw as the novelty of recent developments. He used this particular angle as an opportunity to redouble his message. Community and collaboration are crucial in software development. 'What's new?', Bearden mused:

> ... it is because of the tools that are now available to us that data science can actually become a team sport. We can bring the tooling and the models so that true collaboration can happen ... and that's really the game changer.[1]

This one instance illustrates how ideals of team sport, and other metaphors of collaboration, find their way into Bearden's frequent emphasis, hammering home in fact, of the role of *the community* in data analytics.

This recent event taps into a common theme in accounts of data infrastructures, namely the role of the collective in the constant updating and revising of the various products through which data analytics are conducted. A second key feature is inadvertently captured in Bearden's keynote. The event – an annual summit on Hadoop – had that year been rebranded from the Hadoop Summit to the DataWorks Summit. The reason for the change was their desire to continue to focus on Hadoop but to do this within a context of wider developments in data and software. This rebadging signals the role of Hadoop in the story of data analytics infrastructures and its position as a central component within a transforming and proliferating constellation of tools. Hadoop, as this name change suggests, remains a key point of reference but it is couched within visions of a complex, evolving and constantly progressing infrastructure.

In this chapter I switch attention from the visions and imaginary discussed in the previous two chapters to the codified analytical spaces of the data gaze. In Foucault's *The Birth of the Clinic*, the clinical infrastructure is central in facilitating the emergent medical gaze. The clinical space, including its features and apparatus, were necessary for the gaze to be put to work effectively. The medical gaze, in Foucault's account, was deeply entangled with the material infrastructures in which it was deployed. The clinical gaze was based around the relations between what, at the time, were new analytical infrastructures that operated alongside and were woven into new types of analytical discourse. In this chapter we look at how the data gaze is facilitated and entangled with the very different material infrastructures of data analytics.

The clinic became 'the domain of the careful gaze', Foucault (2003: xiv) suggests, a hive of considered analyses in which there was an 'intensified faith in visual evidence' (Jay, 1986: 182) – a space in which there was propagated an *'invisible visibility'* (Foucault, 2003: 204). As Foucault concludes, it is not simply that seeing finds a new grid for analysis, it is also that 'the forms of visibility ... have changed' (Foucault, 2003: 242). The clinic provided the space within which this type of visibility could be exercised. With the clinic, Foucault claims, 'a domain of clear visibility was opened up to the gaze' (Foucault, 2003: 128). The clinic is the space in which the gaze is able to see. This makes clear the importance of the infrastructure. It emphasises the need for an infrastructure and the architectural means of observation to afford the visibility required (Nettleton, 1992: 109). The emergent infrastructure and space of the clinic led to 'a gaze equipped with a whole logical armature, which exorcised from the outset the naivety of an unprepared empiricism' (Foucault, 2003: 131). This was a space of silence in which seeing was facilitated (Foucault, 2003: 131–2) and in which notions of an advancing analytical knowledge could be realised. The quiet is important: it facilitates this link between the gaze and discourse, with language intervening in the act of seeing only in the peace of the dedicated arena. Silence is needed for the conversion or translation to take place smoothly. It is through this proximity that analysis can occur or where analysis 'lives at an immediate level' (Foucault, 2003: 34). Proximity here is part of the immediacy of the analysis – whereas heightened immediacy happens, or is sought, *without* proximity in contemporary data analytics. Space and infrastructure are crucial in Foucault's accounts, their particular configurations afforded the spatial and temporal dimensions of the gaze. Medical spaces became dominated by the gaze, Foucault argues. All spaces that did not adapt to the gaze were removed or marginalised (Foucault, 2003: 44). As such, the logic of the gaze becomes dominant and pushes out other approaches. The clinic facilitated the 'constant gaze upon the patient' (Foucault, 2003: 65). Before that, Foucault is claiming, 'the medical gaze, whose powers were beginning to be recognized, had not yet been given its technological structure in the clinical organization' (Foucault, 2003: 61). So there is a need for the gaze to be based upon a technological infrastructure in order for its powers to be realised. Understanding the particularities of the spatial and infrastructural dimensions of the analytical space enables the understanding of its relations to the gaze deployed within it.

The two previous chapters were concerned with the discourse and rationalities attached to data analytics, this chapter looks more directly at the deployment of the data gaze within accounts of the material infrastructures of data analytics. This chapter explores the software infrastructures that reside behind the data analytics industry. A key development in this area is Hadoop, as is captured in claims such as the following, which are fairly typical of the overarching positioning of this software: 'For increasingly diverse companies, Hadoop has become the data and computational agora – the defacto place where data and computational resources are shared and accessed' (Vavilapalli et al., 2013). In this case Hadoop is the agora of data, the space in which it can be explored. In another typical instance it is claimed that 'Hadoop has become the backbone of several applications and Big Data cannot be even imagined without Hadoop' (Banerjee, 2014). Clearly Hadoop is a key player and a part of the 'backbone' of data analysis infrastructures. As discussed in Chapter 2, the promises of the data imaginary are embedded in understandings of the software, with frequent claims that echo those we have already heard, such as the claim that 'Big data tools like Hadoop enable industries to best benefit from all the data they generate'.[2]

The Hadoop software project is widely used across the industry in various adapted forms. The scale of use of Hadoop and its popularity in the analytics industry became clear during the research conducted for Chapters 2 and 3. Hadoop was a frequently discussed package that was often central to the descriptions of the services and data solutions offered. This software is often adapted and reworked by the organisations active in data analytics. Therefore, Hadoop provides a useful case study for understanding the infrastructures of data analytics more broadly, especially as they work their way into organisations of different types. It is also a useful focal point for exploring how the gaze is cast through these infrastructures. There are other software packages that are used, but Hadoop is both an industry leader and a key reference point in descriptions of the broader infrastructures. Hadoop is not a fixed entity, it is an ongoing project that is constantly being updated and revised. However, as this intimates, there are also newer analytics packages on the market that are in some cases usurping or extending Hadoop. This chapter will discuss Hadoop in the context of these other competing developments to give a sense of the data assemblage that is in action and how that assemblage is said to transform data into knowledge. I will then extend the analysis of the previous chapters by linking the envisioning of the power of analytics more directly to the properties of the material infrastructures, the functionality of the software and how these are narrated and described. Using an archive of documents, accounts and guides, this chapter will look at the development of Hadoop over time, and will offer a set of insights into the properties of the analytics infrastructures through which the data gaze is afforded.

Here I draw upon archival work in which Hadoop was tracked through various source materials. Various searches were used to uncover the trail left by the development of Hadoop. The focus began with Hadoop, the trail then led in a number of different directions. The result is that the chapter mushrooms outwards to reflect the way in which the focus on Hadoop led to insights into a mutating analytical infrastructure in which new packages evolve out of the old. The chapter moves through various stages, starting with the technical detail and functions of Hadoop, and then working through how that infrastructure is seen to adapt. It then looks at the changing and splintering analytic environment. In short, it thinks about how this codified clinical space is splintering, adapting and mutating. It looks at new packages and how they are differentiated as well as what they offer to the data gaze and how they enable the data gaze to be applied. The aim is to see how the professional discourse of the data gaze is cemented in understandings of the changing analytical space or infrastructure in which it is deployed.

The hope is that by doing this we can explore the emergence of a key analytic platform whilst also getting a broader picture of the infrastructure of which it is a part. Starting with Hadoop enables an exploration of how it is adapted and shaped in various ways by those engaged in analytics, whilst giving a broader sense of the codification of the analytic spaces of the gaze. The searches produced a vast range and volume of documents.[3] These documentary traces varied in form, from user guides and product descriptions to user accounts, descriptions of adaptations and applications, technical specifications, licence agreements, industry newsletters, release schedules and updates, along with features and functions as captured in provider specifications and manuals. These documents all shared a focus on describing the data infrastructures. The documents were sorted to capture key themes, which then revealed how the entry point of Hadoop opened up not just the features of that particular package but also a network of packages and analytical possibilities. These traces were pursued in trying to understand how the infrastructural dimensions of the data gaze were embedded in those accounts of the infrastructure. More specifically, in this chapter these documents are examined with a particular interest in the way that the material infrastructures are associated with the data gaze.

In the same way that the medical gaze described by Foucault needed its clinic, the data gaze also requires a material infrastructure and analytical space. They just turn out to be very different in their form. The properties of the clinic were seen, by Foucault, to be crucial to the authority of the medical gaze. Its properties were part of the discourse and understanding of the gaze and its analytical scope. Similarly, the infrastructures of the data gaze are central to both its authority and what is understood to be its potential and revelations. The key difference here is that whereas the clinical space was geographically located, demarcated and fixed, the data gaze is performed in more mobile, transient and unbounded spaces. The data gaze may have moved to a codified clinic yet its infrastructure is still central to the performance of the gaze and how it can be understood. Understanding Hadoop is not just important for understanding data analysis, it is also crucial for understanding the very data and media infrastructures within which we now live.

DISTRIBUTION AND COORDINATION

Named after a child's soft toy,[4] for a single software package Hadoop has a fairly circuitous genealogy.[5] A product or project of the Apache Software Foundation, Hadoop, or Apache Hadoop,[6] originated between 2006 and 2007. To be more precise, despite having developed over a longer period, the exact birthdate of Hadoop is often pinned at the 28th January 2006.[7] This moment is framed as a shift towards more collaborative software infrastructures for 'big data'. Rather than providing software for users, which is presented as a model from the past, this alternative drew on what is described as a background in the 'hacker tradi- tion' where developers wrote software to use on specific problems and often for their own use.[8] Accounts suggest that its development was driven largely by the coder Doug Cutting, who began a related project in 1997 and moved to the Apache Software Foundation in 2001 (for this account of Cutting's involvement see Bonaci, 2015; Harrison, 2015; Metz, 2011; Woodie, 2015). In a series of infographics released in 2016 to celebrate the '10th Birthday' of Hadoop, Cloudera claim that they had reached over 1.7 million lines of code in the Hadoop core.[9]

Linked to the earlier Apache Lucene project, which was an open source pro- ject launched in 2000, and the Nutch project from 2004, Hadoop began to emerge (see Harris, 2013). In what is a frequently retold story of a key partner- ship, Doug Cutting worked with Mike Cafarella[10] to develop Nutch. Whilst doing this the pair also looked into potential future products (Bonaci, 2015; see also Harrison, 2015: 28). Wanting to take advantage of the emergent possibilities of distributed analysis, where computational power is managed across a number of machines, and the potential availability of the 'execution engine' MapReduce, that could handle 'large scale data analysis',[11] they set about furthering their collaborative project. This combination started in the Nutch project, which was a 'web crawler' (Bonaci, 2015), but was further and more effectively operationalised through the Hadoop project (Singh et al., 2015: 4634). Following Nutch, Hadoop was launched in 2006 and was functioning by 2007 – giving it a fixed date of birth as well as a period in which it was refined into a functioning tool. In a summary of the development of the history of Hadoop, Derrick Harris (2013) notes that it was only through some persuasion that commercial support was secured for the nascent project. Who has contributed what and how much code since then has become the source of some contention (see Harris, 2013). This gives a time frame and sense of the ongoing difficulties behind the growth of large-scale data analysis.

The emergence of Hadoop is embedded in developments around the distribution of computing power. The importance of the ability to distribute data storage and analysis across devices is often central to these accounts – we might also think of this distribution of the analytic infrastructure as affording a kind of distribution of the data gaze. Distribution created capacity by enabling devices to work together and larger scale infrastructures to function. Within these infrastructures the Hadoop Distributed File System (HDFS) is evidence of the need for the controlled distribution of data (for a description of its place within the 'Hadoop architecture' see Harrison, 2015: 29). There are many descriptions, accounts and guides to the widely used HDFS. The following provides an example of how HDFS is seen to be an extension of previous database technologies and how it works with HBase to impose structure and to order the stored and distributed data:

> While HDFS allows a file of any structure to be stored within Hadoop, HBase does enforce structure on the data. The terminology of HBase objects seem pretty familiar – columns, rows, tables, keys. However, HBase tables vary significantly from relational tables with which we are familiar. First, in each cell – a column value for a particular row – there will usually be multiple versions of a data value. Each version of data within a cell is identified by a timestamp. This provides HBase tables with a sort of temporal 'third dimension'. Second, HBase columns are more like the key values in a distributed Map of Key : Value pairs than the fixed and relatively small number of columns found in a relational database table. Each row can have a huge number of 'sparse' columns. Each row in an HBase table can appear to consist of a unique set of columns. (Harrison, 2015: 32)

The data are ordered for the gaze to be trained upon, this ordering even has a temporal dimension (see Chapter 3). The data are also laid out across a large area in ways suggested to facilitate the scope and depth of the gaze – to look below the surface and into the data. The emphasis upon enabling the data to be seen from other angles is central to the idea that this lifts the surface of the analysis beyond two dimensions. Crucial here is how the data are distributed. It is not just the data that need to be structured and ordered in these distributed systems, that very act of distribution means that these distributed devices need to be *managed and overseen*. This creates a space for the provision of the oversight of distribution and for managing the performance of distributed computing. The data gaze watches over its own infrastructures. The result of this is that providers step into this space to create 'supervisor' software that manages distributed computing. The aim with this type of service is to make oversight automated[12] – and thus to exercise an automated gaze upon archiving and data flows.

The HDFS enables 'distributed storage' for Hadoop which then enables 'distributed processing'.[13] HDFS allows for 'nodes' to be connected in networks of computers, with data then split between them in smaller 'blocks' that are distributed throughout the devices that make up the cluster.[14] As such it is 'designed for scalability'[15] and to cope with large data sets that may be 'structured, semi-structured, unstructured – without any upfront modelling'.[16] Hadoop facilitates the use of servers in large clusters, adding processing power and storage, as well as, it is claimed, increasing reliability. These claims of scale and power are made despite it being able to be run on inexpensive hardware.[17] Distribution does not only require management it also requires delegation, with choices about which devices handle which data and which bits of the processing. MapReduce is the component used by Hadoop to delegate or assign work to these connected servers.[18] The 'coordination' of the distributed system is seen to be paramount and is the focus of a range of innovations and discussions (see, for instance, the discussion of the role of YARN in Harrison, 2015: 31). Harrison (2015: 31) describes the process of coordination in the following terms:

> The Resource Manager coordinates with the various Node Managers to determine which nodes have available resource. The Resource Manager then creates an Application Manager on an available node. The Application Manager coordinates tasks that run in Containers on the selected nodes. The Containers control the amount of CPU and memory resource the application task may use.

There are many diagrams used across these materials that try to show such steps, stages, phases and flows. There is clearly, this reveals, an attempt to define a kind of division of labour within these systems. The distributed 'data blocks', sent out to multiple devices, are usually around 64MB, with each block being hosted by a different 'DataNode'.[19] When retrieving data, the data are then 'flushed', to use the frequently evoked watery metaphors, between DataNodes in stages along the 'pipeline'.[20] The 'pipeline' is also a commonly used way of describing this structured flow of data blocks between nodes (Tiyyagura et al., 2016: 7). The following chapter explores how managing such pipelines can be regarded as part of the domain of the data gaze. As part of these processes, so as to limit faults or data loss, 'three copies of each block are written to three different DataNodes' (Tiyyagura et al., 2016: 7). This is a built-in backing-up that places an emphasis on preserving and protecting the data.[21] Faults are seen as an inevitable part of a distributed system, so managing them to avoid losing data is seen as paramount. The reliability of the analytical space is, as we might expect, crucial to its perceived legitimacy.

Differentiation of nodes and data blocks within these large clusters is also seen to be crucial in delivering data for analysis. The emphasis is upon being able to combine devices within the cluster, whilst also treating each as an individual part of that network. This is what is described as being the key functions of the 'docker', which provides 'consistency' and 'isolation' within the 'software environment'.[22] The data gaze will need to be able to see across and to isolate.[23] As I explore in the following chapter, the data gaze is exercised on the data infrastructures as well as the data themselves. The isolation aspect of this, such as with YARN, is intended to bring greater security, scrutiny and make faults easier to resolve.[24] The sanitation of the data and the removal of faults is clearly a key feature of this analytical environment. As the data, the focus of the data gaze, are distributed across these computational clusters the focus on limiting loss and managing faults acts to legitimate the space and present it as secure, robust and reliable. A managed distributed system is crucial in enabling the data gaze to see all of the stored data and to avoid loss or faults, and thus avoid delivering an incomplete picture. The analytic infrastructure, the codified clinic, needs to be as leak-proof and sanitary as possible. In a similar tone, elsewhere, the developers behind Pig (which I will discuss later in this chapter) refer to 'debugging the environment' (Olston et al., 2008: 1107). The data gaze is then placed within a secure environment in which the security and cleanliness of data is a central feature (I pick up on the cleaning of data again in Chapter 5). In place of the kind of sanitation described in the clinical space, the codified clinic is also rooted in its cleanliness as based upon the careful management of resources and ensuring that no data are lost. Both though are built upon this idea of protecting the purity of the object under analysis by ensuring the stability and faultlessness of the analytic space.

As a result of this distribution of the data across clustered servers, there is a concern with developing components that help to manage resources and schedule these flows of data. These include projects such as YARN,[25] FairScheduler[26] and ResourceManager.[27] YARN, for example, is described as the 'architectural centre of Hadoop' and as 'the foundation of the new generation of Hadoop'[28] – suggesting that it is the architecture of the resources that is central to how these flows of data are managed (on scheduling in Hadoop see Kamal and Anyanwu, 2010). The infrastructural architecture is based around the organisational affordances of these systems. Distributed systems, because of their networked form, need managing in order for them to lend authority to the gaze. Rather than the analytical spaces being fixed, like the concrete spaces of the clinic, here they are built and rebuilt using the scheduling and distribution of data flows as ordered by these types of components. The analytical space here is a product of how it organises itself. As such, the visible components of the clinical space are lost and replaced with a focus on the stability of these comparatively decentralised and less visible spaces.

AN INFRASTRUCTURE OF PROJECTS

Before looking at this architecture and the components within it in more detail, I would like first to take a step back to focus more centrally on Hadoop itself. Understanding the broader infrastructures and how they are organised needs first a grasp of exactly where Hadoop, as a key component, emerged from and how it developed. Hadoop, it is claimed by the developers, is the realisation of 'a popular open source project that enabled easy, affordable storage and analysis of bulk data'.[29] Elsewhere it is said to have brought 'big data processing within the reach of mainstream IT' (Harrison, 2015: 27). This moment, in 2007, is talked of as being the start of these types of infrastructural properties. From these early moments the Hadoop project was imbued with notions of constant and unrelenting development, of an ongoing project rather than a finished product. It is also associated strongly with the idea that it is a part of a varied and flexible analytical space. These two points are partly illustrated by the typical claim from a Hadoop developer that:

> No single software component dominates. Hadoop is perhaps the oldest and most successful component, but new, improved technologies arrive each year. New execution engines ... and new storage systems ... demonstrate that this software ecosystem evolves rapidly, with no central point of control.[30]

This quote captures some of the key themes that this chapter will discuss, in terms of how the analytic space is understood and framed and the way that these are used to legitimise and authenticate the data gaze. The image used is of a much larger infrastructure built upon Hadoop's foundations. My research gives this some support. I quickly discovered that it would require another book or more to track all the different connections and spin off companies and projects that are involved in this infrastructure as well as all the individual actors involved.

Hadoop itself is distributed through the use of various licences, which, the Apache Software Foundation claim, allows them to provide 'reliable and long-lived software products'.[31] These licences are also used to manage collaborations in this particular 'open source software development'.[32] With regard to coding, contributors do not give up the rights to their contributions and can use their creations for other purposes. At the same time, the foundation has the right to use, distribute and 'build upon their work within Apache'.[33] All contributors of 'ideas, code, or documentation' are required to sign an Individual Contributor License Agreement.[34] The focus here, it is suggested, is on clarity around intellectual property and the ability to 'defend the project'.[35] A crowd-sourced or community-based collaboration affords the development of this analytic space, licences are then used to maintain and distribute this open source software development. In short, this is a very different kind of analytic space to that offered by the clinic.

According to the developers:

> The Apache Hadoop software library is a framework that allows for the distributed processing of large data sets across clusters of computing using simple programming models. It is designed to scale up from single servers to thousands of machines, each offering local computation and storage. Rather than rely on hardware to deliver high-availability, the library itself is designed to detect and handle failures at the application layer, so delivering a highly-available service on top of a cluster of computers, each of which may be prone to failures.[36]

This account of the function of the software prioritises the software over the hardware and the stability of networks and clouds over the potential failures of individual devices. Despite this space being less concrete, the emphasis is still on the stability of the apparatus and its ability to provide a sense of authority to the gaze. This authority has to be achieved despite it being spread out across devices. Indeed, it is this collective of individual devices and collaboration of a community of coders that extends this sense of robust and protected space that offers the data up to the eye. Immediately, in this definition,[37] the analytical space is given authority by its reduction of failure and its promotion of analytic flexibility. It may not be contained within walls but this adds something, it is said, to the security and stability of the platform it provides.

With such shifts, Cloudera, an organisation that has come to be directly involved in Hadoop, have pointed out that Hadoop's use moved from processing towards analytics. As they put it:

> Today, Hadoop is not only used for data processing, but also advanced analytics ... These new challenges include social network analysis and smarter targeting by web and advertising companies, content optimization by a wide variety of publishers and network analysis at media and telecommunications companies.[38]

The interest in smarter targeting and notions of optimisation echoes the features of the data imaginary discussed in Chapter 2, such aims are coded into the infrastructure. Here they are accompanied by the observation that Hadoop advanced the possibilities of analysis, and that it was also part of the advancement of the ways that data were talked about in terms of analytical possibilities. Elsewhere, in the case of SAS, an analytics provider that uses Hadoop, the importance of Hadoop is defined in terms of a series of functional possibilities that it brings. These include features that reflect some of the aspects of the data imaginary discussed in Chapter 2, such as the 'ability to store and process huge amounts of any kind of data', the increased 'computing power' that comes with its distributed model, the protection of the data through 'fault tolerance', the ability to capture data in their unprocessed state, to have this at 'low cost' in a form that can change in size and is 'scalable'.[39] Clearly the data imaginary and the data infrastructure are entwined in the kind of back and forth that Charles Taylor pointed us towards (see Chapter 2). The flexibility of Hadoop means that it is used for variegated purposes that deal with data in different ways.[40] It can, for example, be used to run 'analytical algorithms' as part of the analysis of the stored data – taking on the form of an automated gaze – or another popular use is to draw upon Hadoop to build 'recommendation systems' that analyse the data and 'predict preferences'.[41] The predictive gaze that can see into the future, found in the data imaginary, reoccurs in the infrastructure (see Chapter 2).

In terms of its ongoing development, the list of Hadoop releases shows how the software has transitioned since 2006. It also gives a sense of how Hadoop is an ongoing project that is part of an evolving infrastructure that is expected to respond to and anticipate the demands of those wishing to analyse the data. There were, for instance, seven updates launched in a 10-month period between April 2015 and February 2016.[42] This is an infrastructure based upon rapid updating and a pursuit of ideals. This number of updates shows how the authority of the infrastructure and of the gaze it facilitates are based upon a notion of constant progress and an impulse to update. There were also 14 releases during the 2008 calendar year. This gives a sense of the changing nature of the software and the ideal that is cultivated around the constant honing of its functioning. So, for example, the fairly recent addition of 'streaming analytics' is depicted as being a crucial step afforded by Hadoop and other products. The concept of streaming analytics again takes us to these organic, biological and natural types of discourse in describing data and data processes along with an emphasis upon the need to cope with the constant and expanding flow of data.

Streaming analytics, it is suggested, allows for the analysis of 'data-in-motion' rather than 'data-at-rest', enabling the analysis to take place in 'real-time' and 'enabl[ing] action based on an analysis of a series of events that have just happened'.[43] Immediacy is clearly important here (as discussed in Chapter 3). The data imaginary works its way into the infrastructure in the way that data are spoken about as being in constant motion. The infrastructures are built around this idea and expectation. There is a belief that the infrastructure will facilitate acceleration, which again illustrates how the role of speed in the data imaginary discussed in Chapter 3 seeps into the design and features of the infrastructure and the changes that are pursued. The authority of the gaze as rooted in the infrastructure is based upon its ability to move with the data and to be as quick as possible. Data are not seen as large and fixed, held or contained in storage, they are seen to need an infrastructure that does not, as they put it, rest. This takes us back to the data imaginary described in Chapter 2 and suggests how that data imaginary is central to infrastructural developments – with certain ideals and notions of authoritative knowledge driving how the infrastructure is designed and how it is presented. In this case, as described in Chapter 3, the idea that speed and real-time analysis are crucial to keeping up is central to the way that the infrastructure is refined. A key thing to note here is that this is part of frequent talk of enhancing the infrastructure (see for example Yadav et al., 2014: 510–11). As such, the data imaginary is woven into the infrastructure and the lines of development that are pursued.

ORGANISING IDEALS AND MANAGING INFRASTRUCTURAL PROJECTS: FINDING ORGANISATIONAL AUTHORITY

This might give the impression that something very organic and uncontrolled is happening within these infrastructures. In fact, what happens with the Hadoop project is defined by a series of 'project bylaws'.[44] According to these bylaws it is the Apache Software Foundation that 'holds the trademark on the name "Hadoop" and copyright on Apache code including code in the Hadoop codebase'.[45] As with other products of this foundation, the bylaws tell us, this particular Hadoop project 'operates under a set of principles, known collectively as the "Apache Way" '.[46] The bylaws express this 'way' in relation to a series of defined roles and responsibilities. The production of the software is based around a kind of hierarchy of contributors. There are five specified roles in the project, each is defined by the scale of direct involvement with software development. These five roles are: users, contributors, committers, release managers and project management committee.[47] Users are simply those using Hadoop. The involvement of 'users' does not end there though, it is the feedback that they provide such as 'bug reports and feature suggestions' that contributes directly to software development. A feature of the infrastructure is this idea that users are active in shaping what happens and in feeding back areas for development. Including this in the bylaws shows how the authority of the infrastructure is based upon this kind of interactive approach to development. It also embeds these ideals of community and constant progressive development into the feedback structures through which the project develops.

The second category, 'contributors', are volunteers that offer 'time, code, documentation and other resources'. Illustrating how there is a kind of social mobility in this hierarchy, and suggesting a kind of meritocracy is at play in the community behind the development of the Hadoop project, some 'contributors' go on to be 'committers'. Again, these bylaws include a sense that the individual can increase their involvement and help to drive the vision of the constant forward movement of the project. Committers are appointed by invitation, sign a 'Contributor License Agreement' and are 'responsible for the project's technical management'.[48] Above the committers and providing the first line of oversight and control, 'release managers' work to select and create consensus around certain initiatives within the project so as to ensure that there are enough votes to support its release. This is collaboration with oversight and control – a gaze overseeing a gaze. The structures of collaboration are designed to manage and contain developments and to enact priorities within infrastructural developments. It seems that a sense of authority and expertise is established within this flattened and open organisational framework. In some cases committers go on to be members of the project management committee and thus move to a more senior level of oversight. The project management committee for Apache Hadoop was 'created by the Apache Board in January 2008'. This was the moment when Hadoop became a 'top level project' at Apache – illustrating the point when this particular analytic software began to take hold. The authority of the gaze here is rooted in the way that the infrastructure is built within a collaborative yet highly controlled set of interactions and supervisory relations. It is this control over collaborative development that maintains the authority of the gaze and embeds oversight in the very infrastructure itself.

The project management committee or PMC manages the Hadoop codebase. This places the PMC at the centre of the oversight of the project and the direction it takes. The PMC's responsibilities vary, but they include deciding which products are released within the Apache Hadoop project – they approve all 'releases' – they also maintain and coordinate the collaborations behind the code, handle licensing disputes and maintain the bylaws. By invitation only, the PMC group oversees the project and, as a central point of control, lends authority to Hadoop. There is a clear interest in building trust around this project so that the outputs are also trusted. The PMC has a chair appointed by the board of the Apache Software Foundation. The chair is 'rotated annually' and provides quarterly reports back to that board. This is further illustration of an advanced and highly controlled collaborative project – which is also a projection of a set of organisational principles that are built upon ideals of merit, hierarchical mobility and user feedback. The governance structures appear to be built in a way that also impresses a certain organisational logic onto its products and an air of authority rooted in clear management and constant reflection and improvement. This is where the authority of the gaze is to be found, rooted into the way that the development of the infrastructure is organised. As well as outlining its governance structure, the bylaws also detail how voting and approvals take place and how they should be conducted. It also explains how vetoes work in those circumstances. Similarly, it defines the types of actions that are possible and the form they take, such as code changes, the selection of committers, product releases and the like. It may be a project driven by a community of collaborators, still its governance remains centralised. It is an open project whilst remaining carefully supervised and managed.

The above list of roles, procedures and actions gives a sense of the organisational structures that support data analytics and which lead to the ongoing development of the software. The infrastructures behind the data gaze are a product of the feedback that comes directly from the moments of analysis but are also shaped and reshaped by those involved reflecting on the feedback loops to refine or develop the software. The analytic space of the data gaze then is presented as the product of many hands working to constantly refine the form and function of the software. The legitimacy of the gaze emerges out of the ideals of a collective ongoing project, carefully overseen, that seeks to refine the analytic space and its functionality.

INFRASTRUCTURAL SCALES

In terms of the scale of its use, the list of those who report using Hadoop include a range of highly prominent media and tech companies, including Facebook and Twitter, as well as Spotify and a provider of Amazon's data handling systems. A large range of other organisations draw upon and utilise Hadoop[49] (see also Harrison, 2015: 28). The use of other Apache projects is also widespread. Spotify, for instance, use Apache Cassandra as part of the systems responsible for the 'personalisation' of their music streaming, which is geared towards 'learning … tastes and distastes in different contexts'.[50] The scale of Hadoop use is particularly striking. It has been claimed that:

> Hadoop underpins not only Yahoo, but Facebook, Twitter, eBay, and dozens of other high profile web outfits. It analyses the vast amounts of data generated by these online operations, but it also pumps out data into live public applications. (Metz, 2011)

It is worth noting that Microsoft, Google and Facebook, amongst many others, are named sponsors of the Apache Software Foundation.[51] Its other applications range widely, with even bioinformatics researchers (Taylor, 2010) and other science researchers seeking to manage data and workflows (Ren et al., 2013), and exploring its potential in different settings (Taylor, 2010). The scale of use, this list already begins to reveal, is far-reaching. Hadoop is already an established part of the media and software landscape. The cultural reach of the project even extends to the availability of Hadoop T-shirts, hoodies, caps, bags and mugs.[52]

This chimes with one popular account, provided here by the CEO of a data analytics provider, which suggests that:

> What started as an in-house project at Yahoo has become the de-facto-standard for Big Data processing. It is making deep impacts in industries that historically haven't had Big Data embedded into their DNA, such as finance, healthcare and energy. What's even more impressive is the staggering amount of innovation surrounding Hadoop with the growing ecosystem of software built on top of it. (Stata, 2016)

The story here is that Hadoop started as a project within the large new media company Yahoo, but then picked up in popularity and significance, moving from a side-project to a major international presence in data analytics. Hadoop, in the above account, is the key standard for the analysis of big data. The biological metaphor here is the integration of analytics into the 'DNA' of organisations and organisational structures. The tone recalls the type of data imaginary discussed in Chapter 2 and projects it onto this particular project. Also in the above we can note, foregrounding the later discussion in this chapter, the idea of an evolving ecosystem of data analytics (see for example Douglas and Curino, 2015: 1525; Harrison, 2015: 37; Jha et al., 2014; Luckow et al., 2015; Oliver, 2015[53]). Oliver (2016) talks of how quickly this 'roiling ecosystem' has changed in just one year, suggesting, as a part of this claim, that Hadoop has been 'redefined' in that time. Change and redefinition are core ideas in this sector. These ideas bring with them a change in how analytical spaces are perceived and described; moving from being mechanical, synthetic, contained, concrete and angular to organic, distributed, transformative, growing and interconnected. Note how this idea of an analytical ecosystem and organic organisations is also reinforced in the above quote by the use of the notion of organisational DNA into which analytics can be embedded. Together these indicate a shift in the discursive framing of data.

Putting this aside for the moment, I would like to turn to the question of what Hadoop actually is. The answer to this question is not entirely fixed. It can be defined, it is suggested, in a 'number of ways' (Stata, 2016). The definitions and accounts often return us to the idea of an ecosystem. For example, it is claimed that:

> Hadoop is both an Apache project and an ecosystem of technologies. Hadoop the project was the catalyst for an entire ecosystem of Big Data-related projects which fall under the umbrella broadly called the 'Hadoop ecosystem.' This ecosystem does not stand still. There exists an incredible network of software built on top of Hadoop that exemplifies the staggering innovation surround [sic] Hadoop and is testament to its value in today's data-driven world. This software includes those such as Hive, HBase, and, more recently, Spark and Kafka. And that just scratches the surface of what's out there. (Stata, 2016)

Hadoop is presented as both a component and a catalyst, with its presence triggering all sorts of reactions and productions. The biological and organic themes dominate. The notion of the catalyst along with clouds and ecosystems continues in the explanations of what this software does and the context of which it is a part. Indeed, these metaphors are striking in their prominence – with 'Yahoo spawned Hadoop' (Metz, 2011), the 'data lake'[54] and the like. We also begin to see here this central trope of constant perpetual motion, momentum and change. Within these is embedded an apparent impulse to pursue a changing analytical infrastructure; this impulse underpins even the definitions or explanations of what Hadoop actually is. It does not, we are told, stand still. As I will argue, the authority of the data gaze is based in the notion that its infrastructures are subject to constant change and a kind of pursuit of unending improvement. It is a changing ecosystem of internetworked functions with constant expansion as an integral part of its materiality and logic. This goes along with the layering of complex permeable networks that is also evoked by the ecosystem terminology used. The action of gazing is then guided by the way that the features and functions of the software are to be realised in practice.

THE EVOLVING ECOSYSTEM OF THE DATA GAZE: THE MUTATING ANALYTICAL SPACE

Amongst other things, the above discussion begins to indicate how prominent *the idea of* the 'ecosystem' is in understanding the data analytics infrastructure and the codified clinic. The notion of evolution[55] is also prominent in understanding this changing ecosystem – with the individual components evolving along with the overall ecosystem (Woodie, 2016). Following Hadoop shows how the infrastructure opens up and mutates from such genealogical points. Using a starting point such as this, a little like Scott Lash and Celia Lury's (2007) 'sociology of objects', not only shows how this evolution is discussed but also gives glimpses into how it works in practice. The analytic space of the data gaze is a mutating space filled with mutating software. The idea of an evolutionary drive is at play here – evoking a constant and unstoppable force of evolution of both function and form, with new variations emerging as the conditions alter, niches are created, and new code and new projects are realised. A subplot here is that these complex ecosystems are imbued with the ability to sort out the messiness of raw data. As the developers of Hadoop put it:

> Institutions can explore messy, diverse data sources, perform experiments, and rapidly develop and evolve applications. Data from sensors, social media, and production can be combined to develop insights, inform decisions, and fuel new products.[56]

The pursuit of the ever more complete removal of messiness is central here, with new data sources and an ability to create apps placed at the centre of the drive for change.[57] Here the aims of the infrastructure align both with the data imaginary and with Foucault's observations, concerning the ability of the gaze to pursue the depths of the observed phenomena. The medical gaze, according to Foucault, must travel 'vertically' as well as horizontally, allowing it to 'plunge from the manifest to the hidden'; the gaze here moves 'along a third dimension' (Foucault, 2003: 166; for a discussion see McNay, 1994: 51). The pursuit of the invisible depths we see echoed here. Hadoop can run what Cloudera CEO Mike Olsen refers to as 'analytics that are deep'.[58] Part of the image of a dynamic, diverse and progressive infrastructure is this sorting out of mess and an ability to plunge into the depths of the accumulated data debris. This reflects the key ideas around the uncovering of value or the revelation of truth typical of the data imaginary discussed in Chapter 2. Key to understanding how the evolution of the ecosystem is pursued is an understanding of the notions of mess, dirt, complexity, depth and value attached to the data. The codified clinic aims, it is implied, to allow the data gaze to see ever further into the depths of the social.

As this reflection on the active role of the data imaginary within the infrastructure might indicate, the evolution that is spoken of is not something that just happens, it is also actively pursued and promoted as the desired state of things. An added layer of complexity here is that the talk of evolution is part of what shapes the way that the infrastructures themselves change. Statements like 'in the Hadoop ecosystem, evolution is to be encouraged, and as Hadoop continues to move beyond its internet roots, it is also evolving' (Stata, 2016), are fairly common in the discussion of the infrastructure. They show how evolution is promoted as a desired ongoing state. Evolution is seen as a virtue in data analytic infrastructures. Evolution is both how the infrastructures are understood and how their future is pursued. As a result of this type of logic as well as the burgeoning capital that this industry can tap into, the range of projects escalates and the variety of packages expands. According to Apache's own materials, there are a number of what they describe as 'Hadoop-related projects at Apache': these include Ambari, Avro, Cassandra, Chukwa, HBase, Hive, Mahout, Pig, Spark, Tez, ZooKeeper[59] as well as Oozie, Flume, Solr and Sqoop.[60] This is just from the information provided by Apache Foundation, limiting it to this one foundation, yet the number of possible packages mushrooms quickly (there is probably also something more to be said about the names of these projects). This mushrooming is illustrative of the nature of these analytical spaces: they incorporate a wide range of projects and tools. Despite Hadoop's prominent position, there are vast numbers of other tools and components that either operate alongside it, adapt what it does or provide alternatives. There are numerous mutations of Hadoop and other packages, with individuals and groups tailoring the package to their own agendas – a kind of complex and evolving ecology that is seen to be increasing in diversity of species. Even individual projects are remade, like memes, over and over again as they are adapted and reworked. The idea of a mutating ecosystem is also supported by the type of coding licences (and the protection of the core code) discussed above, where users can adapt particular products with their own code.

The consequence of this mushrooming is that slight variations and deviations are used to demarcate and differentiate the various packages and processing possibilities. Small functional differences are used to demarcate these evolving types and to highlight evolution. As the range of options expands so the processes of differentiation become increasingly granular in their focus (something we will see echoed in the division of labour of those involved in the industry in the following chapter). Capturing this infrastructure is to capture these small technical differences. This in turn highlights the type of embedding of expert knowledge required to fully understand these complex and small differences – the data gaze is based not just in technical analytic skills but in understanding which packages, based upon these differences, are most appropriate for the task at hand. This understanding of the combination of components within the infrastructure relates to expertise and is something I will discuss in more detail in Chapter 5, especially in relation to the role of the data engineer. Here though, for the moment, we can see that there is an expert knowledge concerning the differentiations in software. This demonstrates how expertise is embedded into the infrastructures themselves, especially in the way its components are managed and combined. The detail separating out the different infrastructural components is deeply engrained in how the infrastructure is understood, how it is deployed and how it can be used to project authority. Expertise is based in gearing the analytical space, through the choices around the make-up of that space, so that it suits the type of data gaze that is to be operated or the type of issues and questions that the data gaze is to be aimed at exposing or addressing (this issue is developed further in the following chapter). The data gaze that is to be deployed in the future is never far from the descriptions of the data infrastructures. The software itself may often be depicted as being intuitive and enabling analysis with little technical expertise (see Chapter 2), but the infrastructure is deeply interwoven with technical terminology and insider discourse that is orientated around environmental and biological themes and is steeped in a carefully constructed lexicon of features, functions, tools and technicalities. These form the basis of the differentiations central to that infrastructure and to the expertise required to navigate it. As I pick up in the following chapter, with the data gaze expertise is formed and maintained in the construction, modelling and composition of the infrastructure as well as in the analysis itself.

UNPICKING THE EVOLVING ECOSYSTEM OF THE DATA GAZE

Let me pick out one component within this infrastructure by way of illustration of this analytic ecosystem. YARN was launched in August 2012 to resolve the problem of MapReduce having too much to do – more oversight was deemed necessary. Going back to the issues faced with managing distributed computing,

YARN was designed to manage resources and workflow in the 'data pipeline' – work on this started in 2006 (Bonaci, 2015). Again, the pipeline through which data flows is the means by which the functionality and purpose of this product are described. YARN is illustrative of the additional components that are added as the ecosystem, as it is often described, becomes more complex. With YARN the 'new architecture … decouples the programming model from the resource management infrastructure, and delegates many scheduling functions (e.g. task fault-tolerance) to per-application components' (Vavilapalli et al., 2013: 1). YARN's purpose was to increase the ability to manage the delegation of computation across the clustered devices and to have greater control over the movement and distribution of data across those clusters. Again this illustrates the interest in limiting faults and managing the security, stability and cleanliness of the envisioned data pipelines.

YARN is implemented through a combination of three 'interfaces': the 'ResourceManager', the 'Application Master' and the 'NodeManager'.[61] YARN is intended to add greater separation of the components it oversees so that they can be controlled in more isolated ways. The authority comes from increasing the controllability of the clusters of machines and from increased supervision. These three interfaces, implemented by YARN, communicate together as part of the process of managing the flows of information. A series of suggested 'commands'[62] are available depending on the aims of those using YARN – the point being that it can be configured and deployed in different ways and with the ideal of suiting different aims. Those engineering the pipelines seek greater control. As it is explained elsewhere, 'YARN lifts some functions into a *platform* layer responsible for resource management, leaving coordination of logical execution plans to a host of framework implementations' (Vavilapalli et al., 2013: 4). This then is a component within the infrastructure concerned with managing resources, faults and refining the delegation processes.[63] With distributed infrastructures like these, a key aspect of their functioning is how data and processing are allocated across the clusters of devices and 'nodes' that make them up. Hence there are options for 'partitioning' and creating hierarchies of tasks so that resource use can be limited.[64] Similarly, the Apache Ambari project aims to monitor the clusters that Hadoop creates, allowing them to be managed and configured.[65]

As with other expansions in the range of components for processing data, YARN is presented as solving established limitations and increasing the existing options for combining components together (Vavilapalli et al., 2013: 3). As these are often driven by open source contributions, it is imagined that this ecosystem finds the gaps in its own performance and resolves them – embodied in phrases like 'lessons learned'[66] – pushing it in new directions and escalating the range of options. The drive to hone this aspect of these infrastructures is hinted at by the words that make up the YARN acronym: Yet Another Resource Negotiator. The data gaze's ability to watch over itself is codified in this analytical infrastructure.

These evolutionary details are not presented in isolation, they are situated in relation to the broader ecosystem. Here the gaze is aware of the features that make up the analytic space and keeps an eye on them. Often Hadoop remains central to these contextual details, with new variants being either compared to Hadoop or explained in relation to what they add to Hadoop or the component that they replace. For example, it is said that the 'Emergence of Yarn marked a turning point for Hadoop. It has democratized the application framework domain, spurring innovation throughout the ecosystem and yielding numerous new, purpose-built frameworks' (Bonaci, 2015). YARN is not only an additional resource for managing distribution it is also described here as marking a turning point in the ecosystem, both for Hadoop and in the way that it triggered other evolutionary changes and mutations across the 'ecosystem'. The codified clinic's components are highly relational. You will note that the ecosystem metaphors continue and lend a certain biological certainty to the shifts in the infrastructure whilst also turning data from something inorganic and dry into something organic and wet. As well, of course, as suggesting these developments are beyond any individuals' influence, instead they emerge from the ecosystem itself. This is a space in which change is depicted, by those developing it, as incremental and based upon an understanding of where the features of the system need to evolve and solve problems or enhance the range of possibilities.

For further illustration of this increasing range of options and the push for constant development, Spark is an important case in point. Spark is similarly described in relation to the advances it brings. For instance, it is suggested that 'by including streaming, machine learning and graph processing capabilities, Spark made many of the specialized data processing platforms obsolete. Having a unified framework and programming model in a single platform significantly lowered the initial infrastructure investment, making Spark that much more accessible' (Bonaci, 2015). In this account we find Spark usurping many previous data processing platforms, rendering them 'obsolete' with the increased capacity it brings for visual and rapid engagement with the data. Spark's value, it would seem, is in increasing what is visible to the gaze and how quickly it can stream those data into its vision.

Focusing on Spark allows us to explore the above point further. It has been described in the following terms:

> Apache Spark is an open source cluster computing framework. Originally developed at the University of California, Berkeley's AMPLab, the Spark codebase was later donated to the Apache Software Foundation that has maintained it since. Spark provides an interface for programming entire clusters with implicit data parallelism and fault tolerance.[67]

With its origins in academia, the project was picked up by the Apache Foundation and became embedded in these ideas of computing clusters and what is described as an ability to see data running in parallel streams and with limited faults. It is also suggested that:

> Spark is great for many tasks, but sometimes you need an MPP (massively parallel processing) solution like impala to do the trick – and Hive remains a useful file-to-table management system. Even when you're not using Hadoop because you're focused on in-memory, real-time analytics with Spark, you still may end up using pieces of Hadoop here and there. (Oliver, 2016)

Again the authentication comes through an understanding of how to combine components to create bespoke data infrastructures. Spark's particular purpose is articulated through the ideas of data running in parallel – the gaze has multiple objects to behold. There is a constellation of components at play here, being reworked in a kaleidoscope to create infrastructural patterns. Again, Spark is an ongoing project that is open to being refined and updated – by the crowd and in response to identified limiting factors. The interest is in managing faults and channelling data from their dispersal in distributed clusters to the analytic eye. Spark's particular evolutionary advantage, as it might be put, is seen to be its speed and the fact that it can cope with live data – the logistic regression running times of Spark and Hadoop are compared by the Apache Software Foundation to high-light the acceleration in processing, with Spark on 110 and Hadoop on 0.9.[68] These figures clearly provide an infrastructural embodiment of the type of urgency and speed discussed in Chapter 3. Maintaining the idea that collabora-tion is central to the genuine evolution of the infrastructure, the Apache Software Foundation say that 'Apache Spark is built by a wide set of developers from over 200 companies. Since 2009, more than 1000 developers have contributed to Spark'.[69] There is an element here of a kind of crowd-sourced analytic space, in which the legitimacy of the developments is rooted in the numbers of people involved in contributing to it. This is certainly not a fixed clinical space, but an infrastructure in which participatory crowds shape its constant upgrading. The legitimacy here is not in its fixity, as with the architectures and material proper-ties of the clinical space Foucault described, but in the way that it constantly changes at the hands of many people. This kind of constant change is captured in the assertion that the 'biggest thing you need to know about Hadoop is that it isn't Hadoop anymore' (Oliver, 2016).

With all of these changes to the various components and the overall scene, it is not surprising that there have been steps to understand the evolution that is being described and to look across these transitions. According to the data engi-neer Chad Carson (2016), Hadoop has moved through three stages of development. These three teleological phases are based on the development of the ecosystem of which it is a part. Again this highlights the contextualised and relational forms of knowledge at work, with components understood in relation to each other. These three phases move from minor usage to an established eco-system and then to a new phase in which it is said that 'Hadoop is accessible to all business units, and we begin to see multi-departmental uses. IT organizations now must serve all of these business units, a solution that many call "Hadoop as a Service" or "Big Data as a Service" ' (Carson, 2016). In keeping with the general theme of the constant improvement and evolution of the infrastructural properties of data analysis, Carson suggests that despite these phases, Hadoop 'has not yet reached full maturity' (Carson, 2016; see also Tiyyagura et al., 2016: 4). The notion of maturity is interesting here as it emphasises the pursuit of constant development and again introduces a biological or organic vision of these shifts. In fact, the future of Hadoop is a site of frequent conjecture – illustrating this sense of an ongoing and unrelenting development of the properties of the infra-structure (see for example Hendy, 2015).

According to one of the founders of Hortonworks, Arjun Murthy (in Hendy, 2015), who worked on Hadoop for 10 years, the future will be to develop predic-tive analytics further to allow analysis to go from what he describes as 'post-transactions to pre-transactions'. Of course, this recalls the prophetic fea-tures of the data imaginary (see Chapter 2). The stages of development of Hadoop are used to indicate potential futures and to reaffirm a kind of clamour-ing for progression and expansion across different sectors and different parts of organisations – with the data imaginary filtering into those imagined future stages. In this case it is the pursuit of being ever more predictive. An example of this can be found, in microcosm, in one specific case of an 'offsite hackathon' in which the Barclays Advanced Data Analytics team sought to use Apache Spark to develop a recommendation system. They used 'customer shopping behaviour data to build a personalized recommender system'.[70] Based on this experience, this data analytics team described how:

> Spark allows you to write jobs that can run at small scale on a laptop and at large scale on a cluster … So during the hackathon, we could run tests on our laptops (using the Local Spark Context) and then ship the same code to a cluster if we needed more computational power … we didn't have to build 'toy' models that were then rebuilt to scale. Rather, we could work directly on the full data set with production-quality code.[71]

This demonstrates how notions of scale operate, with distribution creating space for the data. Also this suggests that instead of models that are tested and adapted before being used on the data set, the data gaze is able to be exercised directly on whole data sets – even those going well beyond the memory of even the clusters of servers. The infrastructure here is seen to give depth and breadth to the gaze – allowing it to see the whole and isolate its parts. This is just another indication of how the data imaginary works its way into material infrastructures, shaping how the future of these systems is perceived and also how value is attached.

Murthy further suggests that a likely direction for these developments in analytics will be highly user friendly apps that make the use of this software more mobile. Here an ever more mobile codified clinic is the objective. The overall claim is that as a 'community' they want to 'make it easier for these integrations to be done by someone else – to have them just be done' (Murthy, in Hendy, 2015). So the infrastructure is being designed towards facilitating the data gaze of those without expertise, echoing the idea that anyone can be an analyst as a result of these infrastructures, and that the analysis can be performed anywhere, at any time (as discussed in Chapter 2). Similarly, the regular focus on 'trends' in the Hadoop project and other related projects illustrates a reflective tone to the discussions. This interest in predicting future directions, anticipating the pathways of this ongoing change and projecting where things are heading (see for further examples Mackenzie, 2015; Ramel, 2016) is illustrative of the unshakable interest in adaptation, enhancement and ongoing infrastructural change. A progressive drive. The imagined future, as a result, is highly active in these infrastructures.

ECOSYSTEMS, EVOLUTION AND THE EXTENDED GAZE

Inevitably, within this constellation of kaleidoscopic components there are those that are dedicated to the storage and classification of the data being handled and processed. We have already touched on this a little, but there are specific projects that aim to progress this aspect of data processing. Hive, for instance, is described as 'an open-source data warehousing solution built on top of Hadoop' and that 'Data in Hive is organized in Tables, Partitions and Buckets. It supports primitive data types, nestable collection types and user defined types' (Diaconita, 2015: 81). The use of the term 'nestable' catches the eye in this passage and is suggestive of this creation of a safe and secure space in which to hold the data until they are used. The term data warehousing, though, in some ways jars with the more organic, biological and watery metaphors that are more often used, perhaps this is because it is a term that bridges across from an earlier period in data processing (see Chapter 5). Part industrial part natural, this is the discourse of the codified clinic. It seems, though, to capture the combined storing and ordering processes that are going on in Hive. The way that data are classified and archived is inevitably important, in this case in 'tables, partitions and buckets'.

The origins of the greater need for storage and ordering are important here. Making the Hadoop platform accessible to non-programmers and those *pressed for time*, Harrison (2015: 35) has suggested, was at the heart of the design of storage and ordering projects such as Hive. By addressing these issues, Hive's presence meant that Hadoop was opened up to a much wider range of users. For this task Facebook developed Hive, and Yahoo developed

Pig (Harrison, 2015: 34; I will discuss Pig a little further in a moment). Harrison explains that the:

> ... Hive metadata service contains information about the structure of reg-istered files in the HDFS file system. This metadata effectively 'schematizes' these files, providing definitions of column names and data types ... Commands are translated into Hadoop jobs that process the query and return the results to the user. (Harrison, 2015: 34)

The aim of these developments was to increase the number of people who are able to perform a greater range of tasks (Harrison, 2015: 35). You might recall that accessibility was noted as a key feature in the earlier discussion of the data imaginary (see Chapter 2). This pursuit of accessibility is clearly a driver here. The aim was to increase the range of people able to engage in data processing whilst also increasing the number of potential things that could be done with those data. Of course, this interest in classification and metadata illustrates how these infrastructures pose questions that link to the broader issues of classifica-tion and 'classificatory struggles' (Tyler, 2015). It is with developments like Hive and Pig that classificatory systems expand and where the infrastructure makes possible a range of new possibilities for categorisation and classification. The categories or grids of the data gaze are concretised in the features and functional-ity of the codified clinic.

A key development, as might be expected, is the extension and elaboration of an ever greater set of analytical possibilities. A recent development to the analytical capacities of the infrastructure, which is couched again in notions of simplicity, especially with regard to the language used in its coding, is Apache Pig. Apache Pig, which is an 'open-source project in the Apache incubator' (Olston et al., 2008: 1100), again a biological metaphor, is concerned very directly with facilitating the data gaze in terms of affording the analysis of stored data in more direct and diverse ways. In this description Pig acts directly to extend the data gaze's analytical potential. The developers describe this pro-ject in the following terms:

> Apache Pig is a platform for analysing large data sets that consist of a high-level language for expressing data analysis programs, coupled with infrastructure for evaluating these programs. The salient property of Pig programs is that their structure is amenable to substantial parallelization, which in turn enables them to handle very large data sets.[72]

Parallelisation is the crucial feature highlighted here. This returns us to the idea of parallel data use (see also Olston et al., 2008: 1102). Data running alongside one another but connected by Pig, these are infrastructures of scale and multiple flows of information. It suggests that more than one flow of data can be used simultaneously and be fed directly to the data gaze. The data gaze may then be seeing across data sources and parallel streams as it applies its grids and reaches diagnoses (for more on diagnosis and the gaze see Chapter 5). The data gaze, facilitated by the codified clinic, looks across parallel streams of data. The key idea here is that greater amounts of data are brought into focus and made available to the data gaze – with scale and size often equating to the objectivity and accuracy of that gaze (for a discussion of the potentially misleading ideas around scale and objectivity see boyd and Crawford, 2012). When it is not limited to operating upon a single stream, the data gaze can look across streams to find patterns. A greater range and volume of data are then exposed, simultaneously, to the gaze. The ability to see across vast data and find patterns is crucial to the type of knowledge and the analytical descriptions that the data gaze pursues. The aim of parallelisation is to pursue the objective of increasing the range of data presented to the analytic eye.

The developers of Pig continue by adding that:

> Pig's infrastructure layer consists of a compiler that produces sequences of MapReduce programs, for which large-scale parallel implementations already exist (e.g., the Hadoop subproject). Pig's language layer currently consists of a textual language called Pig Latin.[73]

The development of its own language is part of how the parallel streams are rendered manageable and relatable – bringing a new dimension to the relations of words and things (as explored in Foucault, 2003: xiii; and discussed in O'Farrell, 2005: 58; and Kearns, 2007: 208). This remains quite abstract as a vision, but compiling and connecting streams of distributed data to enable them to be analysed together is the emphasised property of the analytical infrastructure. The creation of a language is illustrative of how connections are forged between components that then connect together in differing combinations in these data infrastructures. Along with the pursuit of scope for the data gaze, the corollary pursuit of a more integrated analytic space is demonstrated by Pig. These components are often bound together around Hadoop. In this case 'Pig is a data flow language that runs on top of Hadoop … [and] Pig Latin, a data flow language and a run time environment to execute the data flow instructions' (Pola, 2015). Extending the earlier point concerning the need for carefully managed distribution and delegated tasks, the extended infrastructure also requires communication between components to enable the parts of this codified clinic to work together.

Developing this binding further, the software engineers behind Pig Latin, who were all based at Yahoo! Research, have claimed that this new language they labelled Pig Latin was 'designed to fit in a sweet spot between the declarative style of SQL, and the low-level, procedural style of map-reduce' (Olston et al., 2008: 1099). The knitting together of the infrastructure is seen as crucial to the effective use of the data, a more tightly bound assemblage is clearly an objective of the more dispersed codified clinic. A broader point is that a new type of language was needed to enable these vast imbricated components to communicate with one another. Distribution of computing requires modes of communication that hold together the parts. Some order and coherence needs to be imposed and acts of translation are needed. As this further explanation of Pig illustrates, there is much organisational work to be done as the infrastructure becomes more complex, dispersed and as the risks fracture:

> ... a Pig Latin program is a sequence of steps, much like in a programming language, each of which carries out a single data transformation ... In effect, writing a Pig Latin program is similar to specifying a query execution (i.e. a dataflow graph), thereby making it easier for programmers to understand and control how their data processing task is executed. (Olston et al., 2008: 1100)

It seems that despite talk of a more organic and fluid ecosystem it is the familiarity of a step-based approach that is appealing. An eagerness to build up trust in the codified clinic never seems to be far away in these developments. The objectives and the way that they are described often orientate around notions of a robust and integrated infrastructure. The data gaze, like the clinical gaze, needs an infrastructure that it can trust to present the object or body under analysis within its vision. It is important, for these developers, that the object being observed is not distorted, contaminated or obscured. We have two very different types of clinic when we compare the codified clinic to the clinical spaces described by Foucault, yet both are founded on similar and particular principles of affordance, stability, function and focus.

Pig also speaks to the need for the gaze to be able to roam across data to locate the issues of importance, before then glancing and focusing in on its targets. Pig has several such 'features that are important for our setting of casual ad-hoc data analysis by programmers' (Olston et al., 2008: 1100). The ad-hoc analysis that it facilitates is geared towards this type of gaze that can scan across in order to then drill down into the issues and anomalies that stand out. Key to this, again, is a process of isolation that enables data to be reconfigured to suit the ad-hoc direction in which the gaze is then cast. The infrastructure of the data gaze evolves with its stated need to roam. In this case Pig's 'data model' consists of 'four types', which are:

> Atom: An atom contains a simple atomic value such as a string or number ...

> Tuple: A tuple is a sequence of fields, each of which can be any of the data types ...

> Bag: A bag is a collection of tuples with possible duplicates. The schema of the constituent tuples is flexible, i.e. not all tuples in a bag need to have the same number and type of fields ...

> Map: A map is a collection of data items, where each item has an associated key through which it can be looked up. As with bags, the schema of the constituent data items is flexible, i.e., all the data items in the map need not be of the same type. (Olston et al., 2008: 1102)

In each case the four types within this data model are imagined as material objects that can be separated out as distinct entities within that model. Each of the four break down the processed data to enable an isolated and targeted glance (see Chapters 3 and 5) as well as allowing the gaze to look across broader patterns and fields. The above also indicates the desire to work and process data on different scales and for those scales to be accessible to the gaze. The volumetric vision of the gaze is worked into the infrastructure in these multi-scalar steps.

MANAGING THE MESS AND COMBINING COMPONENTS: CLEANING UP THE CODIFIED CLINIC

The rawness of data is an often-cited concern. Raw data are an unsanitary presence in the codified clinic. Their presence calls for attention and immediate sanitation. A sense of cleanliness equates with analytical legitimacy. When discussing data and infrastructural projects a premium is frequently placed upon 'cleansing and enriching' (Pola, 2015). Perhaps unsurprisingly, it is the rawness of unprocessed data that is contrasted against a cleaned-up version (see Gitelman and Jackson, 2013). The codified clinic cleans and scrubs its objects of study. It seeks an ever greater sense of cleanliness. As one engineer explains, Pig can be applied to carry out:

> ... research on Raw Data: Analysis of raw data used to be carried out by adhoc SQL queries or specialized tools which may submit SQLs internally. Schema is not generally known in raw data, Pig can rightly fit in such scenarios as it can operate when schema is not known, incomplete or inconsistent ... to analyse the petabytes of data where the data doesn't conform to any schema. (Pola, 2015)

Pig is linked in this excerpt to the ability of the data gaze to make sense of the chaos and to locate insights from masses of data – to see into piles of data and find value. Pig is associated with an ability to take the raw data and to refine and process them. The data gaze is attached to an infrastructure that is said to enable it to cope with data that lack coherence and order. The data gaze then is built around the idea that, drawing upon these infrastructural properties, it can bring order to chaos and find patterns in mess. Associated with this is the idea that the data gaze does not need a fixed objective but can roam across these piles of data identifying what matters rather than arriving with a pre-existing analytical focus. As we will see in the following chapter, this feature of the infrastructure is what gives the data gaze its diagnostic and puzzle solving properties: properties that are central to how it is rendered legitimate as an approach to social analysis and ordering. Features like Pig provide an infrastructural basis that justifies the presentation of the data gaze as being able to cope with rawness, to cover surfaces and depths.

The above begins to illustrate the fragmenting of components within the data processing and analytics assemblage. Yet, as has already been noted, Hadoop often remains a key anchor point within those infrastructures – pointing at continuity within the constant pursuit of change. The method I have used, of following Hadoop, may be one reason why it appears so central, but at the same time the connections with other products often loop back to Hadoop. It is commonly noted, for example, that Hadoop was a key foundational development whilst it is now Spark that is in the 'ascendance' (Oliver, 2016; see also Ramel, 2016). The questions are posed in typically evolutionary terms. Commonly this is about what will be the future or what will usurp or disrupt the previous order, as is captured in simple questions like: 'is Apache Spark going to replace Hadoop?' (Mohammed, 2015). This idea of one usurping the other, with the arrival of new developments like Spark, is fairly common (see for example Brust, 2016). Tez, to give another example, moved into the Apache 'incubator' in early 2013 and was seen to provide a similar extension to the possible combination of components and possibilities for enhancing the framework used in data processing (Wolpe, 2014). Tez is described as an evolution of the frameworks offered by MapReduce (Diaconita, 2015: 81). Again, the emphasis is placed upon overseeing the data gaze. This poses a question about what features enable this usurping to take place. Spark is, Oliver (2016) also claims, much faster than Pig. It is likely, he adds, to push it off his future lists of crucial components. Echoing the data imaginary discussed earlier, it is the speed of processing that is seen to be the crucial point of differentiation. Spark, as already discussed, is a 'framework for performing general data analytics on distributed computing clusters like Hadoop' (Mohammed, 2015). It runs on top of Hadoop to allow for 'real-time stream data' (Mohammed, 2015). It is this development of 'real-time' – and the promises of real-time – that is seen to give it the edge and make it speedier. The quicker component usually wins out. It is also this promise of the real-time, as discussed in Chapter 3, that creates the conditions for the data gaze to glance and to respond in the moment (I will return to what this means for practice in Chapter 5).

If we look at the broader themes exemplified by such details, then it is notable that the constant shifting and realignment of components becomes part of how the ecosystem is understood, with new lines developing that advance the possibilities and allow, importantly, for new combinations of components and a more flexible infrastructure based upon new options for mixing and imbrication. As such it is both the potential for achieving the dreams of the data imaginary and also how they fit into the imagined ecosystem that is of importance. We are told, for instance, that:

> Spark isn't only obviating the need for MapReduce and Tez, but also possibly tools like Pig. Moreover, Spark's RDD/DataFrames APIs aren't bad ways to do ETL and other data transformations. Meanwhile, Tableau and other data visualization vendors have announced their intent to support Spark directly. (Oliver, 2016)

Competing in the ecosystem, this is a kind of survival of the fittest. A kind of evolutionary sense of change is dominant in which new variations usurp the old as their properties are honed to suit the environment and its demands. Discussions of which component is best for which type of job are frequent, as are outlines of which combination of components allows for what combinations of actions. These features and guides quite often revert to the discourse of speed and acceleration discussed in Chapter 3. Below is a typical description of the way components fit together, in this case focusing upon HBase:

> HBase is a perfectly acceptable column family data store. It's also built into your favourite Hadoop distributions, it's supported by Ambari, and it connects nicely with Hive. If you add Phoenix, you can even use your favourite business intelligence tool to query HBase as if it was a SQL database. If you're ingesting a stream of data via Kafka and Spark or Storm, then HBase is a reasonable landing place for that data to persist, at least until you do something else with it. (Oliver, 2016)

This indicates the type of integration, relationality and combination of components that is common in building the infrastructures from which analysis can be performed. It is in the combination of components that the authority of the infrastructure is based. The components are of value where they connect 'nicely'. Components that act in isolation are not seen to offer much to the infrastructures of the data gaze, it is all about how they work together to create a platform for that gaze. Illustrating its applicability, HBase has reportedly been used by Santander to provide a 'Spendylitics' app that customers can use to analyse their own debit and credit card use.[74] The bespoke fitting of the components to the task is where the expertise plays out and where the data gaze's authority is built out of the bits – as it was for the clinical gaze in Foucault's (2003: 8) accounts, in which the body is analysed in bits rather than as a visible whole. It also indicates how expertise is associated with having the right type of knowledge of how to combine the components for maximum effect (this is something that will be revisited in Chapter 5). And again, this point is couched in organic metaphors of intelligence and ingestion.

To extend this point and to reflect more on how the messiness of data is tidied by the infrastructure – making it pliable and ready for analysis – it is worth dwelling for a moment longer upon HBase. HBase, as mentioned above, is part of Hadoop and is a non-relational NoSQL database, as opposed to a relational SQL database (Wodehouse, 2016). Hadoop, we are told, can work with either type of data (Luckow et al., 2015). This is a crucial distinction in how data are used in these infrastructures. They allow for combinations of different types of distributed data and for data with no structure that can then be combined, even where the aims of their use or analysis may not be clear from the outset. This means that Hadoop is based around a non-relational database in which the relations between data are not structured into the database but can be found later and in different combinations. The above sections have already discussed how the ordering of data is aimed at being structured whilst also allowing the gaze to roam and find targets for analysis. Here the possibilities of the data gaze are located in the way that data can be combined. The gaze does not initially need to work within the confines of the associations made between different data. The data gaze is then freed up to roam across data and to analyse and use those data in different amalgamations. This analytical space is designed then for the data gaze to be able to work across data, to find patterns and to locate insights. It also lends to the vision of the distributed component based constellation type infrastructure of data analysis.

A further illustrative case of the building of escalating infrastructures can be found in Tez. This is a component that has already been touched upon in illustrating the growing complexity of these infrastructures, but we can also focus upon it to further develop the above point concerning the processes of structuring data flows. The software developers behind Tez, in a paper introducing its features, say that it is intended as an:

> ... open-source framework designed to build data-flow driven processing runtimes. Tez provides a scaffolding and library components that can be used to quickly build scalable and efficient data-flow centric engines. Central to our design is fostering component re-use, without hindering customizability of the performance-critical data plane. (Saha et al., 2016: 1357)

The description is of scaffolding for the data infrastructure. A frame holding the parts together. Tez is a framework for bringing components together in the infrastructure, for ordering this proliferating ecosystem and managing combinations of different software together. It holds the components of the codified clinic together. The focus again is upon the way that components are assembled, with Tez providing a framework or library of existing configurations for the components and the data flows across these clusters.

Tez, the developers add, is intended as 'a reusable, flexible and extensible scaffolding that can support arbitrary data-flow oriented frameworks, while avoiding replicated functionalities' (Saha et al., 2016: 1357). In short, it is how the infrastructure can be used to enable an open and free data gaze whilst also allowing order to be imposed upon chaotic data formations – the scope increases.

This is an infrastructure that is defined by its aim to manage chaotic data and to clean up data so that they can be gazed upon in ways that are regarded as reliable and effective. In terms of the assembled components, the role of Tez is not to drive the systems but to provide the framework or heuristics for the data flows to be managed. As is explained, 'It is important to clarify that Tez is a library to build data-flow based runtimes/engines and not an engine by itself' (Saha et al., 2016: 1357). This is a demarcation of functions and roles within the flows of data whilst also suggesting the symbiotic role that is played within the ecosystem. Crucial here is the understanding, or the pursuit of the understanding, of the relations between the components in these systems (something that will be a crucial point in the following chapter). As is illustrated by this observation:

> Apache Tez is an extensible framework for building high performance batch and interactive data processing applications, coordinated by Yarn in Apache Hadoop. Tez improves the MapReduce paradigm by dramatically improving its speed, while maintaining MapReduce's ability to scale to petabytes of data. Important Hadoop ecosystem projects like Apache Hive and Apache Pig use Apache Tez, as do a growing number of third party data access applications developed for the broader Hadoop ecosystem.[75]

Managing and enabling the crafting of the entanglement of components within this imagined 'ecosytem' is the function of Tez – again, illustrating how an ordered and well-composed analytical space is depicted as being crucial to the casting of the gaze and also to the management and negotiation of data, which are depicted as raw, messy and chaotic before their treatment. Also, there is the focus upon ensuring all data are included without the restrictions of predetermined analytical categories, classifications or conclusions getting in the way of the need for a free roaming data gaze to perform its analysis. We might think of this as the construction of a veneer of objectivity.

Similarly, according to Tiyyagura et al. (2016: 9):

> Tez is an embeddable and extensible framework that enables easy integration with YARN and allows developers to write native YARN applications that bridge the spectrum of interactive and batch workloads. Tez leverages Hadoop's unparalleled ability to process petabyte-scale datasets, allowing projects in the Apache Hadoop ecosystem to express fit-to-purpose data processing logic, yielding fast response times and extreme throughput. Tez brings unprecedented speed and scalability to Apache projects like Hive and Pig, as well as to a growing field of third-party software applications designed for high-speed interaction with data stored in Hadoop.

It is worth noting that these are data scientists speaking of this software, not the commercial bodies involved in its production or marketing – showing how the discourse spreads across the sector. As is replicated elsewhere with claims like:

'Tez helps make Hive interactive'[76] and that further Tez support systems were also developed, such as 'Cascading' for data flow and 'Datameer' for analytics,[77] integration is one of the key foci of these infrastructures.[78] It is about increasing the iterations and finding ways to enable the components to work together in ever more compatible and variable combinations. There is a kind of *imperative to integration* in the formation of these components and infrastructures. The motif is that the more integrated the larger the possibilities and the broader and deeper the clustering of distributed servers and data. In short, the greater the integrations the broader the gaze. As such, integration across these distributed systems brings with it the issue of being able to manage those resources and to manage the data flows through these 'pipelines'.

These pipelines can then be visualised, in these systems, in the form of a flow graph – a 'complex directed-acyclic-graph of tasks for processing data'[79] – which allows the distributed data to be visualised in their movements and then recalled. Again, the infrastructure of the codified clinic allows the gaze to watch over itself. Tez, for instance, 'also offers a customizable execution architecture that allows users to express complex computations as dataflow graphs, permitting dynamic performance optimizations based on real information about the data and the resources required to process it'.[80] As well as the data themselves, *the data infrastructure is also subject to the data gaze.* As this description indicates, Apache Tez:

> … models data processing as a data flow graph, so projects in the Apache Hadoop ecosystem can meet requirements for human-interactive response times and extreme throughput in petabyte scale. Each node in the data flow graph represents a bit of business logic that transforms or analyses data. The connections between nodes represent movement of data between different transformations. (Tiyyagura et al., 2016: 10)

The management of the data distribution and pipeline then also becomes subject to the data gaze. It watches the form that its own analytical space takes, turning this analytical space into a codified clinic. The material infrastructure also becomes the focus for analysis and monitoring. Tez offers opportunities for the data gaze to be targeted at the flows of data within pipelines (which I pick up on in the following chapter with discussion of the role of the data engineer). Visualising the flow of data is seen to be important in managing the analytic space properly and in ensuring that it is appropriately delivering the data upon which the gaze can then be exercised. Within these infrastructures the data gaze takes on a kind of *double focus*: it watches the data but it also observes the pipelines and combinations of infrastructural components that deliver those data.

The terminology used here shows how a whole vocabulary has emerged for describing what is going on within these infrastructures and the different components that are combined to make it up. The components themselves are all described in distinct ways, but there is also a dominant discourse surrounding these infrastructures and how their form and processes are described – along with the notions of progress that are then attached to them. The crucial thing here is that to gain its authority the analytical space must be managed, its components must be correctly combined, it must always be explicitly exploring whether it is configured correctly and what might be done to extend the gaze that it facilitates. This is why there are distinct ways of envisioning the infrastructure to complement the envisioning of the data. Many of the developments in the wider ecology of data processing are centred around speed, streaming, security and the limitation of faults. The greater distribution, management of resources and control of clusters is central to how those changing infrastructures are developed and validated. In terms of its structure, as well as seeking to constantly evolve the codified clinic, the data gaze is based upon a distributed and dynamic analytical space.[81] It is in this dynamism that its authority is constructed, rather than in the fixed and material spaces of the demarcated and concrete clinic.

CONCLUSION: THE CODIFIED CLINIC AND THE AUTHORITY OF THE DATA GAZE

In this chapter Hadoop provided a way into exploring the analytical spaces of the codified clinic. The pathways soon started to fork off from that entry point. As this chapter reflects, the infrastructure is far from simple. It is distributed whilst being highly coordinated, varied and mobile. I have only begun to touch upon the array of software tools and projects that are available or underway. Hadoop provided a prominent case but ended up leading into discoveries about the emergence and diversity of these systems. Understanding the analytical spaces of the data gaze requires such entry points to begin to see inside the terrain.

As this chapter has shown, the analytical spaces of the data gaze are often described as being transient, changeable and evolving. Indeed, part of the very authority of the data gaze, part of its professional standing, is based on the idea that its infrastructures are rapidly progressing. More than this though, it is based upon there being an always-explicit impulse for progress and evolution. This type of infrastructure is based on the pursuit of *the next model* and the always-pressing advancement of capacities and components. Standing still is not seen to be fitting with this type of knowledge formation. Instead, it is about the next version, the next tool, the newest type of insights, the expansion of processing power, more oversight, cleaner data and so on. The data gaze is most authoritative, or is seen to be at its most authoritative, when it is based in transitioning techniques, technicalities and adapted constellations of components and tools. This clinic is always on the move, always attempting to expand its capacity and always pursuing an idealised version of knowing, in which the gaze has ever greater scope, intensity and depth of vision. The next version, the next iteration, the next adaptation, are always on the horizon. The result of this imperative to progression is that the data gaze is deployed in what is depicted as a transforming infrastructure. The data gaze can only really be understood with this vision of its infrastructure in mind. The facilities are not stable with fixed material properties, like the clinical space Foucault was analysing in *The Birth of the Clinic*, it is shifting, its features are changing and what it offers in the way of function is never quite fixed. The other outcome of this is that the infrastructures being used to facilitate the data gaze are varied and imbricated. Hadoop may have led the market, but even then it was being adapted, tailored and shifted into bespoke versions. Alongside this, alternative software was being developed by the same and other providers. Foucault's accounts conjure the image of a tiled and institutionalised clinical space; with the data gaze we would always need to pay very close attention to the version of the analytical space that is being used in particular contexts. The codified clinic of data analytics is far from being a homogeneous or standardised entity. The authority of these analytical spaces comes from them being bespoke. In the case of the data infrastructures described in this chapter, the division of labour of the components within the analytical space is paramount and is a key focus in differentiating the roles of the various components as well as the ways in which they can be combined. It is also here that an expert knowledge of these divisions of labour and component constellations is afforded. The authority comes when the infrastructure is envisioned as being a neat, stable, functioning ecosystem that is able to locate and evolve from its limitations.

As these analytical infrastructures of the data gaze have become more varied, mobile and unanchored, so too the possibilities for deploying the gaze have shifted. Part of the professional authority of the data gaze is situated in the accounts of its relative immateriality. Where the clinical space gave authority to the medical gaze described by Foucault, here it is the unanchored immateriality that lends the data gaze its legitimacy. Distribution of processing power is what is central to this. The mobility, anywhere, anytime, always-on type of infrastructures in this discourse are seen to be necessary for capturing the details, performing the analyses and developing the knowledge that is called for by the wider social context. The data gaze is based upon the idea that its immateriality enables it to be responsive, adaptable, agile and strategic. The various analytical packages compete to be the most adaptable, the most integrative, the most mobile, and so on. This shows how these competing infrastructural options seek to place their authority in what their relative and implied immateriality allows (of course, this is not actual immateriality, it is just a different type of material arrangement). The properties of the data imaginary are a frequent reference point in this discourse and in the direction that the infrastructures take. As this suggests, the codified clinic of the data gaze is a much more varied, changeable and dynamic space than the medical clinic Foucault was focusing upon. This also means that the data gaze is authorised in quite different ways to the clinical gaze.

The dominant vision of the codified clinic is of an organic evolving ecosystem. This is a product and expression of a number of agendas. The codified clinic is a complex interwoven ecology of distributed systems and networks. The collaboratively produced nature of the software means that this ecology is a product of many actors and many connected systems and bits of code. This is how this infrastructure is envisioned and conducted, and is the source of its legitimacy. Hadoop might be seen to be a point of origin or a foundation on which much of this ecosystem has been built. It is the growth of the ecosystem that gives weight to the data gaze, along with its pursuit of evolutionary developments. Distributed and co-produced, this pursuit of ongoing complexity and evolution of this ecosystem is how the codified analytic space is legitimised. The functions of the infrastructure are woven into these accounts and facilitate the data gaze in terms of practice whilst also providing the resources for supporting its reach: giving it a terminology and also providing the frame of authentication for the data gaze to be reinforced. The infrastructure both supports and justifies the practices of the data gaze. The infrastructure might make the data gaze possible, but it is pictured as a complex ecosystem that can only be fully known through expertise and insider discourse.

In many ways, the properties of the infrastructures described in this chapter reflect the data imaginary explored in Chapters 2 and 3. This should not be too surprising. One way that this infrastructure is justified and promoted is through those promises and visions. Or, rather, the data infrastructure is promoted as the means to achieving those potentialities and promises. It is as if there is some final imagined version of perfected data analysis and that the infrastructures are now being developed with the unreachable goal of trying to make those visions a reality. The data imaginary informs that ideal, picturing a final destination that can be pursued whilst never being reached. However, the descriptions of this analytical space give us insights into how those promises are translating into techniques, analytics and future adaptations of the software. Understanding the data gaze needs an understanding of both the infrastructure and the ways that the gaze and the infrastructure connect and interact.

What all this suggests is that the data gaze needs a space in which it can be exercised – the gaze is tied closely into the analytical space. It needs tools and prosthetics to be facilitated. The data gaze cannot operate outside of data infrastructures: it is afforded by those infrastructures, their functionality and their direction of development. Those infrastructures are also a product of how the data gaze is imagined and what future possibilities it is seen to hold. The data gaze is not just a product of the infrastructure itself, but of the authority that the infrastructure holds and projects. This is tied closely to the sense that it is always an infrastructure that is under review and under development. There is a legitimacy projected upon it by the impulse to progress and the constant push to evolve the ecology. It gets its authority from being part of a series of updates, adaptations and versions. Starting with Hadoop and then following the various documentary traces has begun to show how this interest in the horizon of possibility is part of what lends authority to the data gaze and shapes the infrastructures that facilitate it. Most of all though, the codified clinic is based upon the principle of oversight, with its structures allowing the data gaze to watch upon its own deployment, processes and distributed structures.

NOTES

1. This talk is captured as part of the opening session of the DataWorks 2017 Summit which is available at https://dataworkssummit.com/san-jose-2017/
2. 'Apache Hadoop at 10', http://vision.cloudera.com/apache-hadoop-at-10/ (accessed 21 April 2016).
3. This chapter and the following chapter use a wide range of documents, some of which are unusual in their format. I do not cite all of the documents consulted as background work for the chapter, instead I cite those that provide particular illustrations that span or capture the broader themes and issues in the documentation. For citation purposes, wherever possible I have used the same Harvard referencing I have used throughout the book. Where this isn't possible, largely because the format of the reference does not fit with the Harvard system, I have used endnotes to describe them and how they can be accessed.
4. 'Apache Hadoop at 10', http://vision.cloudera.com/apache-hadoop-at-10/ (accessed 21 April 2016).
5. There are also quite a few descriptions of what it is and why it is important; for an example see the account offered by the analytics provider SAS, https://www.sas.com/en_us/insights/big-data/hadoop.html (accessed 13 April 2016).
6. The Apache Foundation information was drawn from http://www.apache.org/foundation/sponsorship.html
7. 'A brief history of Apache Hadoop' accessed on Cloudera's official site at http://www.cloudera.com/promos/hadoop10.html (accessed 21 April 2016).
8. 'Apache Hadoop at 10', http://vision.cloudera.com/apache-hadoop-at-10/ (accessed 21 April 2016).
9. 'A brief history of Apache Hadoop' accessed on Cloudera's official site at http://www.cloudera.com/promos/hadoop10.html (accessed 21 April 2016).
10. This story of the collaboration between Cutting and Cafarella is told in numerous places. Sometimes this is told by those who use the software as part of their commercial activities such as SAS, see for example https://www.sas.com/en_us/insights/big-data/hadoop.html (accessed 13 April 2016).
11. 'Apache Hadoop at 10', http://vision.cloudera.com/apache-hadoop-at-10/ (accessed 21 April 2016).
12. An example of this type of provider is Pepperdata, as described in the press release 'Pepperdata achieves latest Cloudera Certification for CDH 5.5 with increased support for Spark on Hadoop', http://www.marketwired.com/press-release/pepperdata-achieves-latest-cloudera-certification-cdh-55-with-increased-support-spark-2098087.htm (accessed 17 July 2016).

13. This is taken from the HDFS user guide provided by Apache Hadoop and available at https://hadoop.apache.org/docs/r2.7.1/hadoop-project-dist/hadoop-hdfs/HdfsUserGuide.html (accessed 6 May 2016).
14. This is taken from IBM's explanation provided in their 'What is the Hadoop Distributed File System (HDFS)?' section, https://www.-01.ibm.com/software/data/infosphere/hadoop/hdfs/ (accessed 6 May 2016).
15. From Cloudera's product guide to 'HDFS, MapReduce, and Yarn', https://www.cloudera.com/products/apache-hadoop/hdfs-mapreduce-yarn.html (accessed 6 May 2016).
16. Ibid.
17. Hadoop's own 'HDFS architecture guide', https://hadoop.apache.org/docs/r1.2.1/hdfs_design.html (accessed 6 May 2016).
18. From IBM's explanation provided in their 'What is the Hadoop Distributed File System (HDFS)?' section, https://www.-01.ibm.com/software/data/infosphere/hadoop/hdfs/ (accessed 6 May 2016).
19. Hadoop's own 'HDFS architecture guide', https://hadoop.apache.org/docs/r1.2.1/hdfs_design.html (accessed 6 May 2016).
20. Ibid.
21. This triple copying, along with the prioritisation of limiting faults and data loss, is also described in Apache Hadoop's guide on how to restart the NodeManager components within the YARN management of the distributed clusters. See Apache Hadoop's guide to 'NodeManager Restart', https://hadoop.apache.org/docs/r2.7.1/hadoop-yarn/hadoop-yarn-site/NodeManagerRestart.html (accessed 6 May 2016).
22. Apache Hadoop's guide to 'Docker Container Executor', https://hadoop.apache.org/docs/r2.7.1/hadoop-yarn/hadoop-yarn-site/DockerContainerExecutor.html (accessed 6 May 2016).
23. For another example of this process of isolation, consider this description of another component called DAG: 'Dag – this defines the overall job. The user creates a DAG object for each data processing job. Vertex – this defines the user logic and the resources & environment needed to execute the user logic. The user creates a Vertex object for each step in the job and adds it to the DAG. Edge – this defines the connection between producer and consumer vertices. The user creates an Edge object and connects the producer and consumer vertices using it.' The above is taken from Hortonworks guide to Apache Tez, second section, http://hortonworks.com/apache/tez/#section_2 (accessed 14 June 2016).
24. From Apache Hadoop's guide to 'YARN secure containers', https://hadoop.apache.org/docs/r2.7.1/hadoop-yarn/hadoop-yarn-site/SecureContainer.html (accessed 6 May 2016).
25. Hortonworks developer's 'Apache Hadoop YARN – Background and an overview', http://hortonworks/blog/apache-hadoop-yarn-background-and-an-overview/ (accessed 6 May 2016).
26. Apache's own guide to FairScheduler, https://hadoop.apache.org/docs/r2.7.1/hadoop-yarn/hadoop-yarn-site/FairScheduler.html (accessed 6 May 2016).

27. Apache's own guide to ResourceManager, https://hadoop.apache.org/docs/r2.7.1/hadoop-yarn/hadoop-yarn-site/ResourceManagerRestart.html (accessed 6 May 2016).

28. Hortonworks developers on the role of YARN, http://hortonworks.com/apache/yarn/ (accessed 6 May 2016).

29. 'Apache Hadoop at 10', http://vision.cloudera.com/apache-hadoop-at-10/ (accessed 21 April 2016).

30. Ibid.

31. Information on 'Licensing of Distributions' provided by the Apache Software Foundation, http://www.apache.org/licenses/ (accessed 13 April 2016).

32. Ibid.

33. Ibid.

34. Ibid.

35. Ibid.

36. 'Welcome to Apache Hadoop!', http://hadoop.apache.org (accessed 13 April 2016).

37. A similar definition that focuses on storage and processing power is provided by the analytics provider SAS, https://www.sas.com/en_us/insights/big-data/hadoop.html (accessed 13 April 2016).

38. Cloudera's discussion of how Hadoop can be applied can be found at https://blog.cloudera.com/blog/2011/09/hadoop-applied/

39. This account offered by the analytics provider SAS is typical of the type of features of Hadoop that are seen to have been transformative to data infrastructures, https://www.sas.com/en_us/insights/big-data/hadoop.html (accessed 13 April 2016).

40. There are numerous accounts of what Hadoop is and what it can do; I refer to a number directly in this chapter, but another illustrative example can be found in the article 'Hadoop: What it is and how it works', http://readwrite.com/2013/05/23/hadoop-what-it-is-and-how-it-works/ (accessed 21 April 2016).

41. A list of different ways that Hadoop can be applied are offered by the analytics provider SAS, https://www.sas.com/en_us/insights/big-data/hadoop.html (accessed 13 April 2016).

42. This information is taken from Hadoop's records of their software releases which is available at http://hadoop.apache.org/releases.html (accessed 6 November 2016).

43. This is taken from an editorial from insideBIGDATA that provided a 'Guide to streaming analytics', http://insidebigdata.com/2016/03/23/insidebigdata-guide-to-streaming-analytics/ (accessed 31 May 2016).

44. 'Apache Hadoop Project Bylaws', http://hadoop.apache.org/bylaws.html (accessed 13 April 2016).

45. Ibid.

46. Ibid.

47. Ibid.

48. Ibid.

49. This detailed list of those using Hadoop can be found at https://wiki.apache.org/hadoop/PoweredBy (accessed 26 June 2017).

50. This information is drawn from Spotify's 'labs' section, which includes information about the software they use. In this case it is an article on 'Personalization at

Spotify using Cassandra', https://labs.spotify.com/2015/01/09/personalization-t-spotify-using-cassandra/ (accessed 31 May 2016).

51. The list of sponsors of the Apache Software Foundation can be found at http://www.apache.org/foundation/thanks.html (accessed 26 June 2017).

52. The full range of Hadoop merchandise can be found at http://cafepress.com/hadoop (accessed 21 April 2016).

53. I could have continued with this list as this is the dominant trope and appears very frequently.

54. From an account offered by the analytics provider SAS, https://www.sas.com/en_us/insights/big-data/hadoop.html (accessed 13 April 2016).

55. These terms are widely discussed and this chapter highlights a number of examples of their use. A further instance of where evolution and ecosystem are used together can be found in *Virtual Strategy Magazine*'s account of 'An evolving market ecosystem', http://www.virtual-strategy.com/2016/05/05/securing-big-data-infra-strcutures-evolving-market-ecosystem#azz47sgjk1gK (accessed 6 May 2016).

56. 'Apache Hadoop at 10', http://vision.cloudera.com/apache-hadoop-at-10/ (accessed 21 April 2016).

57. See also CEO of Cloudera, Mike Olsen's, account of the problems that Hadoop can solve, which concern the ability to solve the problem of having lots of complex data, available via O'Reilly media, http://www.oreilly.com/ideas/what-is-hadoop (accessed 21 April 2016).

58. Ibid.

59. 'Apache Hadoop releases'. A list of releases is available on the Hadoop site, http://hadoop.apache.org/releases.html (accessed 13 April 2016).

60. The list provided by the analytics provider SAS covers the same list of components that can run 'alongside' or 'on top' of Hadoop plus the additional three at the end of the list, https://www.sas.com/en_us/insights/big-data/hadoop.html (accessed 13 April 2016).

61. Apache Hadoop's 'high-level' guide to implementing YARN 'Hadoop: Writing Yarn applications', https://hadoop.apache.org/docs/r2.7.1/hadoop-yarn/hadoop-yarn-site/WritingYarnApplications.html (accessed 6 May 2016).

62. Apache Hadoop provide a series of suggested 'YARN commands', https://hadoop.apache.org/docs/r2.7.1/Hadoop-yarn/Hadoop-yarn-site/YarnCommands.html (accessed 6 May 2016).

63. There is a lot of coverage of enhancements and how these enable greater management of resources and clusters, such as in the coverage of Commvault software enabling Hadoop. This was covered in various places including at Networks Asia, http://www.networksasia/article/commvault-software-now-enables-hadoop-greenplum-gpfs-big-data-environments.1458487712 (accessed 13 April 2016).

64. From Apache Hadoop's guide to 'Using CGroups with YARN', https://hadoop.apache.org/docs/r2.7.1/hadoop-yarn/hadoop-yarn-site/NodeManagercgroups.html (accessed 6 May 2016).

65. Taken from the Apache information about the Ambari project, https://ambari.apache.org/ (accessed 6 May 2016).

66. From Cloudera's information on the use of HBase by Santander Bank, https://blog.cloudera.com/blog/2016/05/inside-santander-near-real-time-data-ingest-architecture-part-2/ (accessed 31 May 2016).

67. A number of these projects have detailed Wikipedia entries, suggesting that these cultures align. This definition is taken from https://en.wikipedia.org/wiki/Apache_Spark (accessed 2 June 2016).

68. From Apache Software Foundation's guide to Spark, http://spark.apache.org/ (accessed 2 June 2016).

69. Ibid.

70. Cloudera software developers reported on this development, with the account provider by those involved in the hackathon, http://blog.cloudera.com/blog/2016/05/the-barclay-data-science-hackathon-using-apache-spark-and-scala-for-rapid-prototyping/ (accessed 31 May 2016).

71. Ibid.

72. Apache Software Foundation's guide to Pig, 'Welcome to Apache Pig', https://pig.apache.org/ (accessed 2 June 2016).

73. Ibid.

74. From Cloudera's information on the use of HBase by Santander Bank, https://blog.cloudera.com/blog/2016/05/inside-santander-near-real-time-data-ingest-architecture-part-2/ (accessed 31 May 2016).

75. Hortonworks guide to Apache Tez, 'A framework for YARN-based, data processing applications in Hadoop', http://hortonworks.com/apache/tez/ (accessed 14 June 2016).

76. Hortonworks guide to Tez, section 3, http://hortonworks.com/apache/tez/#section_3 (accessed 14 June 2016).

77. Hortonworks guide to Apache Tez, fourth section, http://hortonworks.com/apache/tez/#section_4 (accessed 14 June 2016).

78. For an illustration of this focus on integration, take for a further example this account of Tez: 'Apache Tez provides a developer API and framework to write native YARN applications that bridge the spectrum of interactive and batch workloads. It allows those data access applications to work with petabytes of data over thousands of nodes. The Apache Tez component library allows developers to create Hadoop applications that integrate natively with Apache Hadoop YARN and perform well within mixed workload clusters.' Taken from Hortonworks guide to Apache Tez, 'A framework for YARN-based, data processing applications in Hadoop', http://hortonworks.com/apache/tez/ (accessed 14 June 2016).

79. Taken from Apache's own description of their Tez project, http://tez.apache.org (accessed 14 June 2016).

80. Hortonworks guide to Apache Tez, 'A framework for YARN-based, data processing applications in Hadoop', http://hortonworks.com/apache/tez/ (accessed 14 June 2016).

81. The dynamic visualisation of data and of clusters is crucial in this construction – seeing data flows so they can be managed, such as with Apache Tez's use of 'dynamically reconfigured graphs'. We can see the value placed on dynamism in passages such as this: 'Distributed data processing is dynamic, and it is difficult to determine optimal data movement methods in advance. More information is available during runtime, which may help optimize the execution plan further. So Tez includes support for pluggable vertex management modules to collect runtime information and change the dataflow graph dynamically to optimize performance and resource utilization.' Hortonworks guide to Apache Tez, second section, http://hortonworks.com/apache/tez/#section_2 (accessed 14 June 2016).

$$\boxed{5}$$

The Diagnostic Eye: The Professional Gaze of the Data Analyst and the Data Engineer

> I look for someone who is willing to look to take data and make it sing.
> (A company CEO talking about data analysts)[1]

In the early 1980s, as part of a thought experiment, the data processing expert D.R. Howe conjured an imaginary manufacturing company, Torg Ltd. Howe was interested in using this imaginary company to explore the possibilities of combining data analysis with database design. Howe (1983: 3) used this 'mythical' manufacturing company to ask 'what is non-redundant data? Why share it? What problems arise in sharing data and how can they be overcome?' The imagined company, we are told, proceeded with some caution, aware, as they were, that 'many pitfalls await the unwary in the development of computerized systems' (Howe, 1983: 3). As a result, they start by simply using a database system to produce an up-to-date product catalogue. A wise move perhaps. Yet it is a move that contrasts sharply with the clambering data-centric enthusiasm captured in the visions of the data imaginary discussed in Chapters 2 and 3. Such a shift from a cautionary to an unflinching embrace of data has moved those responsible for data-led processes to centre stage. In those early and tentative ruminations, Howe suggests that data analysis can be understood as 'the properties of the data which exist independently of the transactions which may operate on the data'; this he then distinguishes from 'functional analysis' which is 'the analysis of the transactions which the data model must support' (Howe, 1983: 156). In Howe's reflections, which describe the role of analysis in database systems, there is an early attempt at the separation of the analysis of data from the analysis of data systems and their outputs. We see then that the terminology and differentiation of the analytic gaze has been a concern since the fairly early stages of computerised data use and data-led processes. In these early accounts of the expansion of computerised and data management systems, there reside some of the origins from which our current circumstances have arisen. This is most notable in accounting for the division of labour in data systems and the interwoven relations between the analysis of these systems and the analysis of the data those systems store and deliver.

Writing in the mid-1970s, a few years before Howe's thought experiment, the computer scientist S.M. Deen (1977: 184) noted that:

> ... the introduction of a data base as the central reservoir of data affects the user organization in a number of ways. For example, it changes the organisation's attitude to data requirements and management, it creates new authorities and it brings in new skills.

A change in attitude towards data and the emergence of new skills, these are identified as the key changes that are likely to arise. Again, the watery metaphors of Chapter 4 reoccur in the description of data – giving some sense of the longer history of such comparisons. This also reveals that the data gaze has a history and is based within a genealogy of data analytic actors. Organisational structures have been reshaped by these data-centred systems since at least the 1970s, with the roles and practices of actors morphing and developing since that time. The above passage suggests that the arrival of these data systems brought with it new types of skills and created new authorities. Those that had a legitimised knowledge and an aptitude to work with the data took on a new and more prominent role in organisations, especially where these organisations began to reshape themselves and bend to the presence of data. Deen saw this as a change of perspective as well as a shift in practice. He felt that it was necessary that the arrival of these new database systems would also bring about a reorientation in training – people needed to reconfigure their thinking, this suggests, to fit the new order. This 'reorientation course', he contended, 'should be designed not only to teach the staff new skills, but also to reorientate their outlooks as dictated by the needs of the data base' (Deen, 1977: 185). The data gaze is not just about a shift in technique, it is also a shift in outlook. The data gaze began to establish itself in such moments of organisational reorientation. Indeed, one data warehousing expert has suggested that this type of professional 'information processing' has only really existed since the 1960s (Inmon, 1996: 1), meaning that the moment of reorientation has been unfolding for some 50 years or so.

More recently, it is said that it was the 1990s when data analysis really started to take hold. It was at this time that data analysts really began to take on a profile, particularly as the skills of analysis were seen to have fallen behind the possibilities offered by the data. It was time to address this lag and to catch up. As the Finnish computer scientist Heikki Mannila once claimed:

> The area of data mining, or knowledge discovery in databases, started to receive a lot of attention in the 1990s. Developments in sensing, communications and storage technologies made it possible to collect and store large collections of scientific and industrial data. The abilities to analyze such data sets had not developed as fast … The area can loosely be defined as the analysis of large collections of data for finding models or patterns that are interesting or valuable. (Mannila, 2001: v)

The data analyst becomes more important, in such accounts, than the already advancing systems. The data analyst is depicted as having the ability to unlock the promises and potentials of the data and of these systems. They almost come to embody the data imaginary in this sense. Their role, it would seem, was to work with these new types of proliferating data, to find patterns and to use them to locate value. The geospatial data engineer David Bianco claimed, in an interview, that this escalation of interest in data is even connected to the idea that data are 'more widely recognized as the source of truth'[2] – an observation that clearly returns us to the notion that the gaze produces truth. The difficulties for which the data analyst is developing particular skills, Mannila (2001: v) adds, concerns the vast number of 'observations' in these new data along with the fact that 'data about the real world is seldom' in traditional matrix forms. The 1990s, this illustrates, were associated with the early stages of vast data extractions from 'mundane' life (Hand et al., 2001: 1; see also Simon, 1997: 1). The push, then, was for a vision that could identify 'patterns that involve multiple relations in a relational database' (Džeroski and Lavrač, 2001: vii). Patterns and relations are seen here to be central to this emergent form of knowledge. Especially potent or highly regarded are patterns that are visible across different data sets.

Looking back, where data mining and analysis are concerned there is inevitably a lot of discussion of patterns and how to find them. In the early stages of the field and its development through the 1990s, patterns are given preeminence (see for example, Michalski et al., 1998a). From these early stages, patterns were seen to be central to the new types of knowledge that were pursued through these emergent data (Džeroski, 2001: 8; Hand et al., 2001: 427). Data analysts were already invested in pattern recognition. One of the distinctions made by those sketching out the nascent field of data mining was to demarcate and clarify what these patterns were and what they could be used for. One such account proposed that patterns could be compared to models to add some clarity, suggesting that a 'pattern is a local concept, telling us something about a particular aspect of the data, while a model can be thought of as giving a full description of the data' (Hand et al., 2001: 427). These patterns were located in various forms, such as 'associational rules', 'frequent sets', 'generalizations', 'episodes from sequences', and were to be assessed using 'criteria for interestingness' (Hand et al., 2001: 427–40). The evaluation of *interestingness* seems to indicate that there is an emphasis placed on the judgement of the data analyst and their skills at spotting what is interesting. Elsewhere, the data analyst is encouraged towards slightly more objective or scientific sounding 'query-centered' approaches to data mining (Feldman and Hirsh, 1998: 238) or to using 'vision systems' to find patterns in images (Michalski et al., 1998b). This, amongst numerous other points, indicates that patterns and the data analyst's ability to spot them were central to the knowledge being developed through data – with the data often not being designed, intended or gathered with the purpose of mining in mind (Hand et al., 2001: 2). A wide-ranging view and a diagnostic eye was in demand, especially one that could work in conjunction with algorithms. The problem, then, was not just finding patterns, but finding what would be considered to be 'useful patterns and rules from large data sets' (Hand et al., 2001: 427). The data gaze is charged with finding, judging and reading patterns.

The reflections provided in the previous chapters, outlining the kind of data imaginary and infrastructural dimensions of the data gaze, along with the above discussion of the institutional role of data analytics, lead us to the key figure of the data analyst. The data analyst has been present in the shadows of the last three chapters, both in imagining the data and as actors within the infrastructures, but this chapter seeks to draw out their practices and actions in a little more detail. Here I will seek to examine the way in which the analyst casts a *diagnostic eye* upon the data, drawing inference and conclusions from the data they see.

In this chapter I look across a variety of accounts to see this diagnostic eye in action. Using descriptive accounts and resources, the chapter will begin an encounter with the gaze of these protagonists. In this chapter I will primarily be concerned with professional data analysts and their gaze. This book will argue that the data gaze is something that can be exercised outside of professional practice, but this chapter will explore how certain types of analytic practices reside within those professional spheres and how expertise is demarcated in particular ways. Here, the data gaze is something that is done professionally using techniques and methods that in some way demarcate a professional jurisdiction. This is about the practice of the professional analyst, how they exercise their gaze upon data and how they confer status and authenticity on what is said. In short, this chapter is concerned with how professional analysts cast a diagnostic eye.

Given the importance of intermediaries, as discussed in Chapter 2, it is important to have some sense of these figures. One key aspect of the clinical gaze described by Foucault was the beholder, who, in that case, was a qualified expert. In his reading of Foucault's text, Gary Gutting (1989: 119) concludes that knowledge was folded into a 'right to practice' or as John Gardner puts it, it was possessed by those clinicians who were 'endowed to speak with authority' (Gardner, 2017: 252). Foucault claims that 'once the criteria of competence had been laid down, a selection could be made of those to whom the lives of citizens might be safely entrusted' (Foucault, 2003: 95). There is a clear notion here of qualified expertise and authority, and a selectivity and exclusivity of the gaze. In this chapter we encounter this kind of qualified expert in data analytics. I do this by focusing predominantly on two central figures: the data analyst and the data engineer. Focusing on these allows for comparisons, an exploration of the division of labour and for an examination of the way that the gaze is exercised on both data and data systems (picking up on the double focus of the gaze discussed in the previous chapter). I also use these figures to reflect upon the demarcation of the data gaze across different roles and forms of expertise. We take these as two particularly important figures in the deployment of the data gaze; both train a professional diagnostic glance at the data. The difference here is that we will not see the data gaze as being limited solely to experts, rather these experts deploy it in a particular way, supported by a particular technical know-how and in association with a particular discourse of knowability, calculation, code and built expertise. As the data gaze spreads outwards it takes different forms. The more inexpert gaze, touched on in Chapter 2, relies heavily upon the intuitive nature of the software to facilitate it and to support the idea that anyone can be a data analyst, whereas the expert user of the data gaze relies upon their knowledge of code, tacit understandings of the components that make up the infrastructure and a closer working knowledge of the raw data. The diagnostic eye of the expert data gaze sees that raw data, rather than being restricted to part-baked pre-prepared outputs of the software. This is, in fact, a central distinction in demarcating expertise. To explore the different features of the more expert incarnation of the data gaze, the chapter will draw upon autoethnographic accounts, practitioner videos, interviews, trade publications, technical guides and industry publications, amongst other resources. Let us start first with the figure of the data analyst before then looking at the demarcation of expertise in relation to the data gaze.

THE DATA ANALYST: AN EYE FOR A PUZZLE

The claims made around the power of the data analyst, as with the data analytics themselves (discussed in Chapter 2 and 3), can be quite expansive. The data analyst, as a role, is integrated in the data imaginary. As with the data imaginary, the role of the data analyst is also caught up in the marketing of the services and in the promotion of the potentials of their data analytics skills. As with the infrastructures, the data imaginary and data practices are woven together, rendering them difficult to separate. In fact, separating them would miss something of what is happening and of the interdependencies here. Claims such as 'data analytics for me means harnessing the power of big data'[3] and, even more grandiose, that 'the people who can work with that data will rule the world'[4] are not uncommon. Whilst they might jar, they do suggest that there is a push both to promote the sector whilst establishing what these individual analysts can achieve. The practicalities are weighed against these visions. As the chapter will highlight, the data imaginary mixes with practice and is embodied in these actors.

It is perhaps not surprising that the role of the data analyst emerges out of those commonly held and often repeated notions of data revolutions or deluges. There is a need, it is often claimed, for sense to be made of all of those data. There is the assumption that innate value resides in the data and that it just needs to be pulled out and used. The result is that the figure of the data analyst has moved from the side-lines to centre stage and their practices have expanded to solve, respond to and narrate those data. The data analyst has risen in response to the promises of the data imaginary and is responsible for making real some of that envisioned potential. This is a tough task given the scale of the promises being made. As Jim Gray of Microsoft Research put it in a foreword to a 2001 book on data mining:

> We are deluged by data – scientific data, medical data, demographic data, financial data, and marketing data. People have no time to look at this data. Human attention has become a precious resource. So, we must find ways to automatically analyse the data, to automatically classify it, to automatically summarize it, to automatically discover and characterize trends in it, and to automatically flag anomalies. (Gray, in Han and Kamber, 2001: vii)

In this vision, the increasing automation of the data gaze is the key to unlocking potential. This unlocking requires an infrastructure that allows for automation and a space in which the data analyst's cognitive skills are enhanced by these automated systems. Crucially, the data gaze is required to work within these automated structures whilst also being active in constructing and managing them. To cope with the data deluge, as it is imagined, we need analysts but we also need the agency of those analysts to mesh with machine learning and automated systems – a process that is sometimes actually overseen by dedicated 'machine learning engineers' (Dossman, 2017). When we think of data analysts we should perhaps then be thinking of a human actor interfaced into such active systems, taking us back to the types of cyborg dreams famously discussed by theorists like Donna Haraway (1991) and William J. Mitchell (2003), and perhaps towards notions of a 'posthuman' presence (Braidotti, 2013). This image of a deluge of data is familiar, and has a long history (see Beer, 2016b). In the current incarnation of this story, the data analyst has come to represent a human or human–machine hybrid solution to such a deluge. These figures are expected to create insights through a combination of skill, analytical ability and the capability to know and martial both the data and the analytic tools available. Time pressed and data rich, the analyst's skilled glance is seen to be of great value.

With the masses of data, the inevitable problem is what this skilled glance should be deployed upon. As discussed above, one obvious approach is to find patterns.

The data gaze is aimed at doing more than just finding patterns though, as this account indicates:

> Measures of pattern interestingness are essential for the efficient discovery of patterns of value to the given user. Such measures can be used after the data mining step in order to rank the discovered patterns according to their interestingness, filtering out the uninteresting ones. (Han and Kamber, 2001: 28)

Returning us to this elusive notion of interestingness, again this illustrates how it is such judgements are understood to be central to finding value. If an interesting pattern is located it becomes the key to unlocking value. The data analyst's gaze is aimed at not just finding patterns but recognising 'interesting' patterns. Interestingness appears to be attached most directly to those patterns that suggest anomalies, break with norms or have properties that suggest that they are revealing something usable. This has echoes of the earlier connections between patterns and what is considered interesting, with 'criteria for interestingness' (Hand et al., 2001: 440) being discussed as a way of measuring this value (also discussed in Simon, 1997: 43). Making interestingness the measure automatically maintains or defends an element of human agency, discretion and judgement within these hybrid systems. Finding patterns is part of the data gaze, but so is this ability to measure which patterns are 'interesting'. So, this is not just an eye for a pattern, it is also an evaluation of which patterns, amongst the many, actually matter. There are patterns everywhere; the data gaze seeks the patterns that are important. The scale of the data means that lots of patterns will be found, here the data gaze is used to differentiate, rank and prioritise patterns amongst all this patterning. The aim is not just to find patterns, but to find or filter the right kinds of patterns – clearly then impacting upon the discoveries made and the knowledge that subsequently ossifies.

The interest in the background skills that afford the pursuit of interesting patterns echoes in claims such as: 'Data analysts need to have a baseline understanding of five core competencies: programming, statistics, machine learning, data munging, and data visualization' (Han Lee, 2014). Data munging is another term for cleaning data and is the process of converting data from one type of format to another; it is sometimes also referred to as data wrangling.[5] This can involve looking for bias, or for missing data or for things that 'could be strange'.[6] Such skills are necessary, we are told, because the role of the data analyst is to 'package the data to provide digestible insights in narrative or visual form' (Han Lee, 2014). They mediate, clean or translate the data and make it 'digestible' or render it comprehensible to others. This role of translator is not an uncommon position within which data analysts are imagined. The act of translation is actually central to understanding their organisational roles and the apparent necessity not just to analyse but to make data insights accessible and readable (for a further illustration, see point 10 in Eremenko, 2017). In one guide to becoming a data analyst, it is even suggested that part of this communication of the value of data to other parts of an organisation requires the analyst to employ 'empathetic listening'.[7] Finding the interesting patterns and translating them for others to use, these are two related activities that fall within the jurisdiction of the data analyst. As such, data analysts are said to 'have a strong understanding of how to leverage existing tools and methods to solve a problem, and help people from across the company understand specific queries with ad-hoc reports and charts' (Aghabozorgi and Lin, 2016). This problem solving is a product of how the data are analysed whilst also being concerned with how the findings are made visible and understandable to others who might not be data experts or quantitatively inclined. Responsively producing visual aids and other resources to translate these data, the data analyst is expected to be active in finding value, or interesting patterns, and making this value clear to others. The data gaze is targeted with finding patterns, interesting patterns, and then with imagining how those findings can be presented to make them accessible. The data gaze, as such, pre-digests data.

This has taken us to the end points of these practices and mixes together lots of different types of activities, let us take a step back. The label data analyst is quite amorphous. It covers a lot of different types of work, different types of skills and different roles. This makes it a little tricky to get at exactly what these figures do. They work across different sectors, have different positions within different types of organisations, they work to variegated objectives. The general descriptions that data analysts provide of their own work include claims that their role is 'to help other people in the company to make decisions and prioritise their work by using the data that we collect'.[8] An example given by this particular analyst is to check if particular campaigns are working or to try to gauge the success of a product. The description continues with the observation that, 'everyday I'm working on a new area of the business and I'm helping people do their jobs more effectively by using data'.[9] A mobile and transient form of work that is responsive to the organisational structures, this is what is being described here. Working across organisations with the objective of using data to find improvements and increase effectiveness, the data analyst's gaze may roam. Similarly, their activities and acts of translation shift around with varying objectives and focal points. As it was put elsewhere, the data analyst is 'looking upon data to act on and improve things'.[10] The data gaze, in this account, is deployed on different parts of the organisation but is always charged with honing and developing organisational practices. The eye is diagnostic, finding faults or potential limitations and seeking solutions to those limits. There are lots of illustrations of how these actors seek to overcome such problems at the community site StackOverflow.[11] At StackOverflow data workers post questions about problems and they share potential solutions. It is an active site with high numbers of queries and responses. In this case there is evidence of analysts working collectively to resolve or overcome these types of problems and boundaries. The data analyst then is an agent of competitive development diagnosing and resolving before moving on. Despite this transience there is also a sense of a community of actors with some loose bindings.

Elsewhere the act of continuous problem solving was described as a cyclical process that is repeated in different settings. The analyst is in 'the analytics cycle and it's a never ending loop of acquiring, exploring, visualizing, testing and studying data – and how you can jump from one piece to the other'.[12] The vision is of stages in an analytical cycle that are repeated until the areas for improvement are diagnosed and responded to. The data gaze works in cycles to refine its insights and diagnostics. The analytics are looped in this kind of testing and retesting of analyses.

The nature of these diagnoses and responses is revealing in understanding the data analyst's role. The links that are formed and cemented are between data and value. The data gaze is targeted at locating value within masses of data and using this to locate improvements and prescribe. It has been suggested in one account, for instance, that 'a skill is to look at a data set and understand what is valuable to measure'[13] and that 'being able to look at a data set and understand what is going to be valuable and focus on those things'.[14] Finding areas of value and focusing in on them, targeting them, is something that was a preoccupation even in the early stages of data mining (see for example Hand et al., 2001: xxvii). The data gaze is linked here with a type of targeted value generation. The data gaze is seeking out and foraging for what is valuable within masses of data. The glance is targeted, as Foucault (2003: 149; see also Chapter 3) put it, but in this case it is targeted at value. Quickly calculating what should gain attention and then focusing on that one section or cluster to uncover the limits of value within it. Finding value is not sufficient though, these targets are uncovered with the provocation or stimulation of particular actions in mind. The data gaze does not limit itself to technical diagnoses. The prescriptions come in the form of accessible insights that can be accessible to different audiences. The act of translation is not just in showing what the data reveal but in showing the way those revelations matter and need to be acted upon – hence the data gaze is both diagnostic and prescriptive. The language that accompanies the data gaze is technical but can then also be filtered to facilitate action. It is important, as one data analyst put it:

> ... to take your findings and relay them to different audiences. We don't want to just talk like they need to change something because we said so. We want them to know and understand what we look at, what we found and why it's important to take these next steps to go toward an improvement.[15]

The diagnostic eye is used here to locate value and to explain why the data should be followed. It also captures the ongoing pursuit of 'improvement' discussed in the previous chapter.

The previous chapter discussed the prioritisation of an infrastructure that is secure, that can manage faults and that can deliver clean and sanitary data. The data analyst is expected to work in such ways also. The focus here though, with this hygiene, is upon the protection of value. It has been claimed that a big part of the diagnostic skills of the analyst, or of the skilled expert analyst, is found in their ability to clean and sanitise the data. This fits alongside an ability to get rid of 'bad data'.[16] The diagnostics and value are seen to reveal themselves once the dirt is removed and the data uncovered. The capable analyst, the analyst labelled as credible, knows which data are bad or in need of removal. There remains a sense of an expert feel for the data underpinning this expertise. A data analyst's job, it is suggested, is 'to understand the data, clean the data, write an algorithm and then optimize the algorithm'.[17] Within these three tasks, it is the cleaning of the data that is said to be most time consuming and important. As one analyst has put it, getting a 'clean data feed is not easy'.[18] Following this observation, this analyst provides a pie chart segmenting the time spent in a typical working day, the chart shows that 60.9% of the working day is spent 'data cleansing'.[19] Another analyst claims that '70 to 80% of the job is just to clean up data'.[20] The bulk of the work of the data analyst, in this vision, is the cleaning of the data to make it usable and to reveal what it hides. What we might think of as analytics is a much smaller proportion, as is illustrated by the conclusion that '10% is just in the math'.[21] They add to this that the 'remaining time is about optimizing that algorithm, and it's understanding the output of what it is that they are trying to do, it's understanding the problem and looking at the meaning of the context of that problem'.[22] The analysis only emerges once the data are thoroughly cleaned and the algorithms are honed. We have something like the sanitary clinic emerging in these accounts, with data analysis requiring cleanliness of the data to function accurately – data that remains unsanitary may, it seems, corrupt or mislead an inexperienced gaze. The value then, this account is contending, is in the ability to clean the data. It is in this cleaning that the real skill is located, especially, it is claimed, as 'the math has been around for a long time, the real value of data science is in the data'.[23] In terms of time scale, it is added that 'the math has been around for over 60 years'.[24] This shows how the role of the data analyst is not just in the maths or the algorithmic coding, but in the careful cleaning of the data to render those data visible and ready for the puzzles to be pieced together.

A key way that these practices are presented is in the form of a puzzle. This has echoes from *The Birth of the Clinic*, in which, Foucault (2003: 72) claims, gazing is a process of 'deciphering'. The clinical gaze is a kind of decoding of the body; it is exercised to solve the puzzle it looks upon. The data gaze also aims to constantly solve puzzles, to decipher. It is said that, based upon 'problem solving skills', the data analyst's role is to 'solve different puzzles everyday'.[25] This is often depicted as a skill that is central to data analysis. The data analyst should have, it is suggested, 'an interest in puzzles and putting things together and figuring things out'.[26] The image is of the organisational data providing the basis for organisational puzzle solving. The data analyst is the active protagonist working at the solutions and trying to put the pieces together. The puzzles, it seems, are of a particular type: they are about how to draw more value out of those organisations. The diagnostic eye of the expert data analyst is a problem solving eye motivated by a desire to tackle puzzles. As another group of healthcare-based data analysts describe it, 'you are taking a sheet of numbers and figures and putting together lots of different puzzle pieces'.[27] Another adds that 'You don't need to be a mathematician to do my job, you just need to like to solve logic problems', and another that 'you have to be a little bit of a detective and have an inquisitive mind'.[28] The puzzle is the end in itself. The desire to solve puzzles is the motivator and expectation placed upon the data analyst. The message here is that the diagnostic eye of the data analyst is trained upon the puzzle and putting the pieces together. The data become the puzzle pieces and bring with them a sense that they can be solved or that they carry a pre-designed outcome that can be reached. These puzzles are pieced together to create a narrative. As it has been put, 'when I look at numbers what I see are stories'.[29] The vision here is of the data analyst as detective, solving puzzles and piecing together stories out of the displaced bits (for a discussion of how the body is analysed in bits at security borders, see Amoore and Hall, 2009). The emphasis in this data-informed story telling, as we have seen in the earlier discussion of the emergence of a type of data analytics that can see multiple data types, is upon the ability to offer perspective and range. One description of the role of the analyst follows the path through to this vision:

> There's pulling data out of a warehouse, which usually requires a little bit of coding, and then being able to turn it and slice it and filter it from different angles until you figure out what's really making everything else shift.[30]

Seeing data from different angles is the way in which the data gaze is deployed in this account. This is not seeing the medicalised body from the one angle of the expert eye, or even from the position of 'sensorial triangulation' as described by Foucault (2003: 200), it is instead a gaze that seeks to operate from different perspectives to see connections and leave little outside of its scope. The data gaze might home in on a certain aspect or feature, but it seeks to be able to use that to understand relationality between the parts. The idea here is that the data gaze should be able to see the individual parts whilst also understanding the relations between those parts, placing them within bigger puzzles.

This puzzle solving is built upon a set of fundamental skills, thus puzzle solving is a driver but is also a skill to be acquired. The foundations of such acquired skills enable, it is claimed, flexibility and the ability to move between puzzles, to adapt and to solve their unique features. There is talk of understanding the fundamentals of using basic or even rudimentary packages in developing skills and in showing a flare for dealing with the data without too much algorithmic assistance. This is a hands-on skill that is said to be built up over time, bringing with it the ability to find as well as solve puzzles. It is suggested that this is 'kind of like gardening … getting your hands dirty, working with the data by hand. Having that understanding is incredibly valuable as you progress through the more advanced ways of working with your data.'[31] In a separate guide to becoming a data analyst, this hands-on type of approach to knowledge taken by data analysts is further described in which 'it is not the math (although math is involved), it is not english or accounting. It requires a hands on approach in order to truly understand the pitfalls good analysis will run into.'[32] The point made here is that expertise is built upon a working knowledge of different types of systems, especially basic systems where the analyst cannot rely on automated systems for their problem solving. These skills need to be developed with raw and dirty data that are handled, initially at least, directly and without too much algorithmic interference or assistance. This suggests a kind of status-based adherence to underlying fundamental skills that only expert analysts develop from the ground-up. This fundamental knowledge is central to the expert's diagnostic eye; it forms in these hands-on engagements with palpably raw data – data that are not prepared or pre-analysed by automated systems. The data analyst may have an eye for a puzzle but the suggestion is that the ability to genuinely solve puzzles comes from a direct and working knowledge of the data themselves.

THE DATA ENGINEER AND THE DEMARCATION OF THE DATA GAZE IN PRACTICE: KEEPING AN EYE ON THE LOGISTICS AND BECOMING DATA-SAVVY

Starting with the data analyst perhaps conceals what is seen to be a range of activities conducted by different types of data workers. A focus on 'the data analyst' not only mixes together a range of different roles, it also elides the processes of data analysis in different settings. The rest of the chapter looks to separating out some of these features and roles. One place to start is with exploring how the stages of data analysis are broken down, which in turn then can be used to explore the different roles and divisions of labour that go on within the sector. Extracting or discovering knowledge from data is depicted as being a series of stages that actors follow or intervene in. These stages, some of which we have touched upon, are presented as including steps such as:

1. Data cleaning (to remove noise and inconsistent data)
2. Data integration (where multiple data sources may be combined)
3. Data selection (where data relevant to the analysis task are retrieved from the database)
4. Data transformation (where data are transformed or consolidated into forms appropriate for mining by performing summary or aggregation operations, for instance)

5. Data mining (an essential process where intelligent methods are applied in order to extract data patterns)
6. Pattern evaluation (to identify the truly interesting patterns representing knowledge based on some interesting measures …)
7. Knowledge presentation (where visualization and knowledge representation techniques are used to present the mined knowledge to the user). (Han and Kamber, 2001: 7)

Here we can see how the process and roles start to be demarcated and also see more of the sequential temporality of the data gaze. The sequencing of the stages of data analysis begins to break down the different tasks and suggest how those involved might perform different roles or combine these roles together. In Chapter 3 we saw how sequencing was important to the type of clinical gaze Foucault explored; here we find the sequencing of stages of the analysis even if the data are not then themselves analysed in sequence but from multiple sources and angles. Instead of encountering the data analyst as a single category, this then shows how attempts are made to mark out expertise and to create a division of labour for data workers – with workers then being classified by the stages within which their skills are deployed.

It is revealing to see how those involved demarcate data processes. This is embodied in attempts to differentiate between data engineers, data scientists and business analysts – with various combinations of computer science, statistical skills and 'domain expertise' used to facilitate these distinctions (see for example Schmidt, 2015). In another case, profile data from the social media site LinkedIn were used to show the skills differences between data engineers and data scientists (see Stein, 2016) – with certain statistical techniques identified that data scientists 'need to master' (Le, 2017). This is suggestive of how comparisons are used to draw the lines and boundaries between roles.[33] The conclusion drawn from the LinkedIn profiles was that data engineers are focused more upon infrastructures whereas data scientists and data analysts are more focused upon the data.[34] As I will discuss, the data engineer is responsible for how data are used within organisational structures, both analysing the data whilst also thinking about how the data can be stored and how they can be analysed and utilised within the context of organisational practice. In another comparison, data engineering and data science are seen to combine in support of decision making or 'decision science' (Kwan, 2015). The distinction here is made in terms of background, with the data scientist being said to have roots in 'applied statistics' and the data engineer in 'systems engineering' (Kwan, 2015).

The data engineer role might even be tracked back to what was referred to in the 1970s as the 'Data Base Administrator', who was said to be responsible for the 'creation of the data base, performance optimization, data protection, specification and enforcement of standards, and coordination and the provision of the user facilities' (Deen, 1977: 186). In this short excerpt there is already the language of the management of performance and the importance of the storage, control and protection of data. The roles, this indicates, were segmented from quite early on in the establishment of data processing, storage and analysis. This separation of roles has traces back into the 1970s, but became much more pronounced through the 1990s onwards (see for example Inmon, 1996: 295). Some consensus seems to have been established concerning this separation of roles and the claims to jurisdiction and expertise within analytic processes and structures – although some labels remain contested or seem to overlap. Another way that this type of distinction is articulated is through a notion of 'facilitation', with data engineers enabling the activities of data analysts, data scientists or other protagonists in analysis processes (Insight Fellows Program, 2014). There is a good deal of discussion within the industry about the roles of data analysts, data engineers, data scientists and, sometimes, business analysts (this last label varies a little). A point made here is that 'with the emergence of big data, new roles began popping up in corporations' (Aghabozorgi and Lin, 2016).

With this expansion of the use of data, a classificatory grid of roles began to emerge and take shape. The more complex and wide ranging that the data processes became, the more pronounced and intricate became the separation of roles. These types of roles have a longer history, but with the expansion of data processes the drive to classify the roles has increased at pace. The careers advice offered is instructive here, where it is suggested that 'all that data crunching requires an army of data masters' (Han Lee, 2014; see also Eremenko, 2017). The advice here is that the 'first step on your path to professional data whiz? Taking stock of your three main career options: data analyst, data scientist, and data engineer' (Han Lee, 2014). These classifications often operate around the types of skills allocated to these roles and also to the types of platforms and software with which they are familiar. Here the infrastructure and knowledge of that infrastructure take on a central role in the qualifications of the data gaze. The 'toolkit' is often presented as being defining in the roles (see Han Lee, 2014). The toolkit type definition of these roles illustrates *how the data imaginary, the infrastructure and practices intersect*. The data gaze is exercised differently by these different protagonists. Their position within the infrastructure and their knowledge of that infrastructure form the lines on this grid. For example, in a number of cases the data engineer role is defined explicitly by the 'skills' and 'tools' they use. Lists of skills and tools are used to compare different individuals involved in data analysis: the list for the data engineer includes 'Hadoop, MapReduce, Hive, Pig, MySQL, MongoDB, Cassandra, Data streaming, NoSQL, SQL, programming' (Aghabozorgi and Lin, 2016; see also Han Lee, 2014). This kind of list is not untypical in explaining how these roles differ and shows how the infrastructure explored in Chapter 4 permeates into the demarcation of the data gaze in practice – it also points towards the insider type terminology that creates boundaries around those roles. This type of inside terminology of expertise is demonstrated by this description of such a practice:

> Given an alert, we look at our pre-built Splunk or home-grown dashboards that contain items that we often look for. If we can't find the answer there, we'll often look at our logs loaded into Redshift after different stages of aggregation (event and session level). Sometimes we'll leverage iPython notebooks for visualization. (Irwin, 2016)

Despite the suggestion that anyone might be an analyst, as discussed in Chapter 2, there is a clear demarcation of expertise in this type of terminology. Knowledge of systems and platforms within the analytic space lends credibility to the individual whilst also defining how their gaze may be exercised and what it is that their diagnostic eye aims to reveal. Claims to certain types of knowledge of these systems and certain focal points for the gaze become the defining features of these categorised roles. This type of separation can be found in a number of infographics, in which the roles of data engineer, data scientist and data analyst (and even statistician) are mapped out against a range of criteria. Such infographics are part of the formation of this grid of skills and infrastructural tools as well as the organisational responsibilities of these roles.[35] This leads then to increasingly distinct and detailed separations of the roles within data analysis. Within this grid, the engineer emerges as playing a distinctive role in facilitating the data gaze and, additionally, in exercising their own type of data gaze upon the feasibility of the flow of this 'data deluge' across 'pipelines'.

The Insight Fellows Program (2014), who are involved in providing training for data engineers, say this:

> Our definition of data engineering includes what some companies might call Data Infrastructure or Data Architecture. The data engineer gathers and collects the data, stores it, does batch processing or real-time processing on it, and serves it via an API to a data scientist who can easily query it. (Insight Fellows Program, 2014)

The data engineer then plays the part of ensuring the data reach those involved directly in analysis. This involves managing the storage, in data warehouses, as well as engineering the systems and managing the pathways the data take.[36] In short, they compile and manage the component-based infrastructures (described in Chapter 5), with the aims of achieving the visions of the data imaginary (as set out in Chapters 2 and 3).

Turning to an early user guide on data warehousing, so as to provide some further grounding for this aspect of the data engineer's role, we find it described as a 'home for "secondhand" data' (Simon, 1997: 10) or 'the coordinated, architected, and periodic copying of data from various sources, both inside and outside of the enterprise, into an environment optimized for analytical and informational processing' (Simon, 1997: 12). It is the coordination of storage that falls to the data engineer. In a separate instance the data warehouse takes on a more technical flavour, whilst still being aimed at supporting decision making, with the data warehouse being described as a 'subject oriented, integrated, non-volatile, and time variant collection of data in support of management's decisions' (Inmon, 1996: 33). The data warehouse is an organisationally embedded storage resource from which insights are to be retrieved; as such it needs to be managed and coordinated. The Insight Fellows Program's (2014) vision of collecting and batching conjures images of crops of data that are reaching wholesalers, and fits with these earlier visions of data warehousing. Data engineers serve up the data, in this type of formulation. The language here is of those seeking to provide the right type of inputs into the data analytics process, with this ability then used to evaluate the quality and expertise of the data engineer. This type of evaluation is illustrated by the Insight Fellows Program's guidelines:

> A good data engineer has extensive knowledge on databases and best engineering practices. These include handling and logging errors, monitoring the system, building human-fault-tolerant pipelines, understanding what is necessary to scale up, addressing continuous integration, knowledge of database administration, maintaining data cleaning, and ensuring a deterministic pipeline. (Insight Fellows Program, 2014)

A 'good' data engineer, here, is one that optimises the analytics processes but who is also selecting, shaping and managing these flows of data. Again we have the cleaning of data and the management of pipelines as being the focus of this knowledge and skills. In this case it is referred to as a 'deterministic pipeline'. Unsurprisingly, given the water metaphors surrounding data, data engineers are often understood through these types of plumbing metaphors, combined with an insider terminology around packages and plug-ins. The data engineer role, this metaphor suggests, is in maintaining the functioning of the pipework. The data engineer is judged by their grasp of the logistics. These logistics, in this type of framing, become pipes and flows that need managing or plumbing:

> Data engineering, when limited to ETL, is seen as a question of plumbing. How do you lay out your storage? What data access patterns? How do you address correctness and robustness? What about scalability? Not that plumbing isn't difficult, but the question left un-asked is, 'what does the data science team actually need as inputs?' And in serving those inputs, there is much research to be done. (Kwan, 2015)

The ETL abbreviation used here, which is illustrative of a solidification of jargon, means extract-transform-load, which is reference to the stages through which these plumbed data flow (see also Bemby, 2017). The data engineer has the objective of maintaining data flows within what is understood to be a plumbing system.

Whereas early database management focused on capturing data to have accurate records, here the focus is on flows of different types of data for insights to be located. The types of questions driving the data engineer include '*Is the infrastructure running properly? Is it delivering the data we intended? Is our infrastructure affecting others, with co-location of services or costing too much?*' (Irwin, 2016, italics in original). The vision is of the maintenance of a crucial utilities infrastructure that resides below the surface of data analytics. The plumbing metaphor works to place the data and pipes below the surface of these envisioned spaces.

As this intimates, a very commonly used description, widely repeated, is of data gushing down pipes. In this case it is imagined that a 'data engineer builds a robust, fault-tolerant data pipeline that cleans, transforms, and aggregates unorganized and messy data into databases or datasources' (Han Lee, 2014).[37] The data engineer produces pipelines that are directed to the data gaze – again, cleaning and sorting out any messiness is part of this. The data engineer directs and maintains these 'pipes'. The data engineer also sometimes cleans and tidies the data. The suggestion here is that the data engineer pre-prepares the data, removing its rawness (on data rawness see Gitelman and Jackson, 2013). As such, and echoing the earlier vision of the facilitator, it is surmised that 'data engineers essentially lay the groundwork for a data analyst' (Han Lee, 2014). The data engineer is still part of the production of value through data, but they are rendering data available and in the right state for that value to be mined. Again, these responsibilities begin to solidify into points of contrast between actors:

> Whereas data scientists extract value from data, data engineers are responsible for making sure that data flows smoothly from source to destination so that it can be processed. (Han Lee, 2014)

The smooth transportation of data to the analyst's eye is the focus of the data engineer. This does not mean that data engineers have no data gaze themselves. Far from it. It seems rather that we have different types of data gaze working in collaboration.

To explore this role a little further, we can turn to a particularly detailed autoethnographic account of data engineering. This account explores the emergence of the data engineer as a distinct role within organisations. This tells us something of the new knowledge regimes associated with these expanding processes. In this account, one juxtaposition raised is with the data scientist:

> Like data scientists, data engineers write code. They're highly analytical, and are interested in data visualization ... Unlike data scientists – and inspired by our more mature parent, software engineering – data engineers build tools, infrastructure, frameworks, and services. In fact, it's arguable that data engineering is much closer to software engineering than it is to a data science. (Beauchemin, 2017)

Here we see how the data engineer responds to the need for infrastructural management. Adding to the analysis of the data themselves, the data engineer's gaze is also concerned with the analytical context and infrastructural demands of the data gaze. Building tools and apparatus, the data engineer looks upon the affordances of the frameworks in place. They see the materiality of the organisational context and the data gaze within it. This is a data gaze that oversees the utility of the gaze of others. The utility and mechanisms of the data gaze also then become a subject and part of the analysis. The data engineer is preparing the way and preparing the data. The data engineer, in short, is responsible for managing the analytic space of the codified clinic.[38] This means that the act of analysis is folded into the analysis of the infrastructure.

The importance of preparation of the data is often emphasised in accounts of the data engineer. For instance, it has been claimed that:

> Data Engineers are the data professionals who prepare the 'big data' infrastructure to be analyzed by Data Scientists. They are software engineers who design, build, integrate data from various resources, and manage big data. Then, they write complex queries on that, make sure it is easily accessible, works smoothly, and their goal is optimizing the performance of their company's big data ecosystem. (Aghabozorgi and Lin, 2016)

The work done within preliminary forms of preparation is important here. The engineer is part of a kind of pre-analytics stage of the process. This links directly to the discussion of cleaning earlier in this chapter: here we have the actor actively building, maintaining, cleaning and sanitising the codified clinic (discussed in Chapter 4). The engineer is using the data gaze, or an anticipation of how the data gaze will be deployed, to identify how the data need to be prepared in order for them to be analysed. Again, the data engineer is preparing, this claims, to ensure the smooth working of the analytic process and to 'optimize' the outputs.

Within the data engineer's focus upon preparation the data gaze starts to be elaborated in ways that enable that preparation to occur. It searches around, scanning and moving across data to seek out anomalies, limits and faults; it sees into an imagined future to explore potential scenarios. Like the clinical gaze, it is working across 'aesthetics', finding differences, comparing and contrasting – it 'prescribes the norms' (Foucault, 2003: 149). The data engineer's pursuit of an ideal type preparation is explained in terms of an ability to scan or exercise a roving eye. This is the data gaze in motion, tracking shifts and changes. The temporality emerges again here: it is a gaze that is trying to keep up with the data and with changes in the analytical platforms. As the software engineer Spandan Bemby (2017) explains, 'typically, a data engineer will have strong programming skills and a deep understanding of the big data ecosystem, and distributed systems in general'. Keeping up with the intricacies and new developments of the components described in Chapter 4 is identified as a key to this role and is also how expertise is distinguished. As one data engineer has explained:

> … there is an endless stream of new external technologies and nomenclature to keep pace with. We can pilot a new superior alternative, or try it out in the next company hackathon. Within the organization there is always an evolution on best practices, maybe in security or simplifications in the service infrastructure. Lastly, our team must understand how the organization's needs for our data evolves. Currently, many things are transitioning from daily batch to streaming. (Irwin, 2016)

The diagnostic eye develops in line with notions of 'best practice' and of an ideal means of preparation. There is a sense here of how the data gaze needs to keep up to date with change and be mobile. It is expected to see the infrastructural components that are coming on the horizon and understand how these might be combined. This mobility of the type of data, the social world and the infrastructure is wrapped up with keeping an eye on the future.[39] It is about diagnosing and anticipating what will come from indicators and signs. The same data engineer says that the data gaze is bound to a kind of self-reflection and an envisioning of potential future horizons. He adds that:

> We continually ask ourselves: *Does our current infrastructure meet our needs in the future? Does it scale as site visitors increase and new application features are released?* Often our data needs will drive our infrastructure needs; for example, we might discover the plausibility of a new signal by ingesting more sources of data. (Irwin, 2016, italics in original)

A constant driving curiosity is placed at the centre of data engineering, which in turn has echoes of the drive to constantly progress the infrastructure described in the previous chapter. The idea of a constantly evolving infrastructure also acts to legitimate the individual engineer, projecting authenticity where the engineer is both looking to constantly reshape their use of that infrastructure and where there is a visible drive to progress its functionality. The data gaze comes with an expectation to constantly be imagining future scenarios to ensure that the data preparation, infrastructure and selection are maximised or optimised. This is the unyielding logic that is at play.

Indeed, maximisation and optimisation are key aims of the data gaze, especially as these experts seek to diagnose inefficiencies. A key aspect of this driving optimisation is finding anomalies to be corrected; the gaze here becomes a normalising presence. As the data engineer Ryan Irwin puts it:

> … once the root causes of the anomaly have been identified from our perspective, we evaluate what actions need to be taken. *Should we surface the issue to other teams for additional input? Should we make a fast code change?* If quick code changes are required, having clean coding and testing procedures is key. (Irwin, 2016, italics in original)

The use of the idea of surfacing or bringing to the surface is suggestive of how the gaze plunges into the depths to locate its findings. This surfacing from the depths is, of course, an important part of Foucault's (2003: 204) accounts of the gaze and its vertical sight into the depths, making the invisible visible. This is about the seeking of a kind of hidden truth. Foucault's claim is that 'the clinical gaze is a gaze that burns things to their furthest truth' (Foucault, 2003: 147). The pursuit of clarity in which the 'eye becomes the depository and source of clarity … the eye first opens the truth' (Foucault, 2003: xiv) is evident here. The gaze Foucault describes attempts to see into and illuminate by turning 'darkness into light' (Foucault, 2003: xv). A similar drive to illuminate seems to haunt the data gaze.

The data gaze is deployed to not just find anomalies but to find root causes – the push is to bring these root causes, as they are envisioned, to the surface. Again, this comes packaged with a notion of the cleaning or sanitisation of the data. For instance, it was added that:

> Now that the data has been refined by our MapReduce or streaming systems, we have many alerts that could trigger if anomalies exist. In our case, this could mean that a bug in our logging system is causing mis-classifications, potential abuse on the platform, or a new traffic flow related to new site features. (Irwin, 2016)

Finding such bugs using automated systems is a key component of the data preparation. The anomalies identified trigger actions in how to deal with root causes. Here we have the diagnostic eye in action, identifying abnormalities and diagnosing remedies. The knowledge associated with the data gaze is one which can optimise and render efficient, whilst also fixing, cleaning and bringing issues to the surface. A dynamic and changing infrastructure means that the scope of the gaze widens to take in the infrastructures themselves, keeping an eye on them and ensuring they carry the features crucial to legitimising the insights that will ultimately be produced through them.

This diagnosis, as the above hints, is in some instances attached to a notion of removing bugs. Echoing the earlier discussion of the management of faults (see Chapter 4), the data engineer takes on the role of spotting and identifying where bugs are present. Sanitation is paramount in handling data and the engineer is responsible for managing faults within the codified clinic. This is to remove failures from the system and to ensure that no further bugs remain to infect the outputs of the analysis; it is a question of contamination:

> To address these items we have alerts in place with different tools covering different failure scenarios. As our team grew, we wrote down 'debug and recover' runbooks that emerged as patterns, and when possible we automated parts of the recovery or better utilized our underlying robust service infra. (Irwin, 2016)

The data gaze here finds problems and ways to solve them: it 'debugs' and enables recovery – returning the system or that particular data set to full health. This is seen to be an ongoing and unending process of diagnosis:

> Inevitably, new problems will arise. We've found that defense against this can be helped with thorough documentation of past failures and non-failure-related changes (i.e., descriptive tickets, code reviews). Also, it is key to know your organization's tooling for seeking information. It's been said by many folks at Yelp that *a senior engineer doesn't know all the answers, but they'll know where to start looking*. (Irwin, 2016, italics in original)

Using past problems to find remedies is the way in which new analytic grids emerge for understanding problems, failures and bugs. The engineer, as it suggests here, may not know the answers but they know where to look; as such their gaze seeks out problems and remedies. A diagnostics emerges here that is based upon the accumulation of knowledge about systems and data. It is this knowledge that demarcates expertise.

These various insights into data engineering show how the terminology around this relatively new role of data engineer is deployed. The way that labels are used to create a space for this role is particularly revealing. Aspects of the data gaze are compartmentalised or placed within a grid of analytical roles, showing the variation in the type of analytical practices and notions of expertise behind data analytics. For instance, it is noted that:

> In relation to previously existing roles, the data engineering field could be thought of as a superset of business intelligence and data warehousing that brings more elements from software engineering. This discipline also integrates specialization around the operation of so called 'big data' distributed systems, along with concepts around the extended Hadoop ecosystem, stream processing, and in computation at scale. (Beauchemin, 2017)

By way of a summary, the specialisation of the data engineer is outlined in relation to the need to build and manage functioning systems through which the analysis can take place. The functionality of the ecosystem is part of the role of the data engineer in facilitating the data gaze. The crossover between the data engineer's practices and the infrastructure is obvious here. The analytics of business intelligence combine, it is suggested, with the ordering and management of data storage to engineer the possibilities for analytical insights. The diagnostic eye of the data engineer is cast upon the material limitations of the infrastructure.

The result of this is that the data engineer's role varies depending on the size and type of organisation in which they are located and upon which they gaze (for a discussion of how data mining is performed in organisationally specific ways, see Kennedy, 2016: 137–44). This is captured in the following excerpt:

> In smaller companies – where no data infrastructure team has yet been formalized – the data engineering role may also cover the workload around setting up and operating the organization's data infrastructure. This includes tasks like setting up and operating platforms like Hadoop/Hive/ HBase, Spark, and the like. (Beauchemin, 2017)

This engineer adds that 'in smaller environments people tend to use hosted services offered by Amazon or Databricks, or get support from companies like Cloudera or Hortonworks – which essentially subcontracts the data engineering role to other companies' (Beauchemin, 2017). The role of the data engineer is defined by their ability to engineer and compose the most appropriate platform. The assessment comes from the ability to compose the spaces of the codified clinic. Technical knowledge here is communicated in the references to these platforms. There is an inherent and implied knowledge of what these platforms offer – understanding this is what marks out the expertise of the engineer. The data engineer in these smaller organisations takes the responsibility of choosing and setting up the correct analytic infrastructure. Larger organisations tend to have more bespoke analytic platforms, whereas smaller organisations work with hosted platforms (see Chapter 4). The data gaze here is informed by an understanding of the right type of analytic platform for the organisation as well as the right type of analytics to deploy.

Developing this distinction between larger and smaller organisations, this engineer's account suggests that:

> In larger environments, there tends to be specialization and the creation of a formal role to manage this workload, as the need for a data infrastructure team grows. In those organizations, the role of automating some of the data engineering processes falls under the hand of both the data engineering and data infrastructure teams, and it's common for these teams to collaborate to solve higher level problems. (Beauchemin, 2017)

This gives a sense of how the data gaze varies dependent upon the organisational infrastructure.[40] The data engineer is active in refining and selecting the properties of that infrastructure and therefore in shaping what the gaze is able or expected to achieve. The data engineer, in short, is responsible for integrating the parts that make up the codified clinic. The expert knowledge communicated here is one of an understanding of the properties of platforms and how they can be deployed. Working in small or larger groups to establish data-led processes in different scales of organisations, the data engineer is seeking to implement those moments of reorientation discussed at the outset of this chapter. The way in which analytics are embedded in different organisations is clear here: it is not just the nature of the data or analytics that defines the role of the data engineer it is also the organisational context in which they are operating (see also Bemby, 2017).

Despite these expert and tacit forms of accumulated knowledge, there remains a sense of the spread of the data gaze. As discussed in Chapter 2, the notion of self-service analytics is prominent, attached to particular tools. The data engineer acts to make the spread of the data gaze possible and builds the analytic platforms to ensure that expertise is no barrier to exercising the gaze. As one data engineer put it, 'we now have better self-service tooling where analysts, data scientist and the general "information worker" are becoming more data-savvy and can take care of data consumption autonomously' (Beauchemin, 2017). The spread of an analytic sensibility is attached here to the notion of being *data-savvy*. This type of data gaze is based in the accumulation of a working knowledge of the systems and the data. It is the expansion of experiences of handling data along with tools that enable those data to be handled effectively that has led to this expanding data-savviness. Data, for this engineer, 'is simply too centric to the company's activity to have limitations around what roles can manage its flow' (Beauchemin, 2017). The centrality of data is associated with a kind of flexibility to the data gaze. The vision is of a form of data gaze that is flexible within and across participants and which is central to facilitating adaptable organisations – with the idea being that adaptability with data enables an adaptable organisation. As it is put, 'while this allows scaling to match the organization's data needs, it often results in a much more chaotic, shape-shifting, imperfect piece of infrastructure' (Beauchemin, 2017). The organisational and infrastructural shape shifting is facilitated, in this account, by the amenability of the data gaze and the active glance of the data engineer. The previous chapter has already illustrated how the codified clinic is a space of constant change. Rather than being a fixed form of analysis demarcated clearly by institutional roles, the data gaze we see here is reworked in response to the agendas of that moment. As Claire Maiers (2017) has argued through work in the healthcare setting, it is the institutional context that is important in understanding the type of influence and social implications of data analytics.

In the narrative outlined above, data engineers are working across data systems. This is a gaze that looks down from above, taking in systems, flows and connections. As it is described, 'data engineers are operating at a higher level of abstraction and in some cases that means providing services and tooling to automate the type of work that data engineers, data scientists or analysts may do manually' (Beauchemin, 2017). It is automation that provides the abstraction and distance needed to look down. There is a commonly expressed need to automate, thus the data gaze decides what can be automated and how; it then operates alongside those automated systems. This is illustrated by the claim that:

> … just like software engineers, data engineers should be constantly looking to automate their workloads and building abstraction that allow them to climb the complexity ladder. While the nature of the workflows that can be automated differs depending on the environment, the need to automate them is common across the board. (Beauchemin, 2017)

Again, the pursuit of automation of these systems is a central feature. Automation becomes the ideal, especially in relation to the potential enhancements it brings to the gaze. This again suggests that the data gaze is possessed by or composed of both human and machine, with 'parts of the system to be interoperable with "humans in the loop" who seek to apply manual filtering when necessary' (Irwin, 2016). As discussed in the previous chapter, the data gaze needs its infrastructure but is still seen to be bound up in human agency – with 'humans in the loop'. Machine learning is one way in which automation is understood, with categorisation systems and labelling a key part of how these systems are understood to learn and think. In one case it is pointed out that the data engineer 'also might want to improve our label acquisition practices allowing us to more easily tune our precision and recall for our filters. Improved labeling helps us use more machine learned models as opposed to manually-tuned models' (Irwin, 2016). Clearly then the type of gaze we are encountering here is based in a type of knowledge of how systems think. Automation in these systems means that the gaze takes on a kind of human–machine hybrid. This was always the case but it is to a much greater extent in the codified clinic. The blurring of types of agency is escalating in juxtaposition to manually operated systems; these systems tune themselves but with human input. Not only is the data worker situating themselves within organisations and within the sector, they are also situating themselves within these systems and the levels of automation to which their analysis is exposed.

To move towards a conclusion and reflecting a little more on this act of situating the gaze, we can reflect on the types of lists that attempt to capture the role of the engineer in relation to other data workers and in relation to artificial intelligence. The functions of the data engineer take a very particular form and vocabulary, as the following list suggests:

- data ingestion: services and tooling around 'scraping' databases, loading logs, fetching data from external stores or APIs, ...
- metric computation: frameworks to compute and summarize engagement, growth or segmentation related metrics
- anomaly detection: automating data consumption to alert people [when] anomalous events occur or when trends are changing significantly
- metadata management: tooling around allowing generation and consumption of metadata, making it easy to find information in and around the data warehouse
- experimentation: A/B testing and experimentation frameworks is often a critical piece of company's analytics with a significant data engineering component to it
- instrumentation: analytics starts with logging events and attributes related to those events, data engineers have vested interests in making sure that high quality data is captured upstream
- sessionization: pipelines that are specialized in understand series of actions in time, allowing analysts to understand user behaviors. (Beauchemin, 2017)

This list represents an attempt to demarcate specific tasks that both occupy and afford the data gaze: calculating, finding anomalies, managing tools and instruments, experimenting, controlling the swallowing of data into systems, and handling the temporality of analysis. We see here a kind of clinical discourse in which the practices are defined by the management of the infrastructure that facilitates the data gaze. This is about using instruments and testing so as to deploy metadata grids to find abnormalities and deviations – which should become almost instinctive or a reflex as it becomes trained into practice. As it has been put: 'for a data engineer, entity-relationship modelling should be a cognitive reflex, along with a clear understanding of normalization, and have a sharp intuition around denormalization tradeoffs' (Beauchemin, 2017). Or, as it was put 40 years earlier, 'undesirable associations are removed from a relation by normalization which can be defined as [a] step-by-step reversible process for transforming an unnormalized relation into relations of progressively simpler structures' (Deen, 1977: 135). Normalisation and norms are powerful and defining in the role of the data engineer – finding norms, establishing norms, reacting to norms, making norms seem reliable and objective. Despite variations, many of which this book highlights, there is something here about how the data gaze imports a clinical discourse to authenticate and legitimise its outputs. This would suggest that there is something in the development of the data gaze that calls directly upon the clinical gaze for both its articulation of the practices and systems and to provide a touchpoint for understanding and authenticity. There remains something clinical about the data gaze even if it has been lifted out of the clinical space; it retains some of the same properties in its knowledge, diagnostics and analytical grids. The way data and analytic spaces are spoken of still carries some of that terminology and flavour.

Foucault argued that the clinical gaze is a 'classificatory gaze' (Foucault, 2003: 5), and it is hard to not reach the same conclusion here. The analysis requires the placement of characteristics and features within the spaces on an existing grid. With the developments in the clinic, what was changing, for Foucault (2003: 64), was the grid. It was with the shift in 'perceptual codes' and of the classificatory limits, which meant that 'the whole system of orientation of this gaze also varied' (Foucault, 2003: 64). The result, Gutting (1989: 120) infers, was that this shift involved 'seeing medical objects through a new interpretive grid' – which requires then an analysis of the structure of that grid. These grids and classificatory systems are powerful in shaping what the gaze sees and what it is then used to say. As Foucault (2003: 1379) makes clear, there are then limits and boundaries placed on the gaze: it is not open and unconstrained. There are instead stages through which the analysis moves to apply the grid and the ideals of description that the grid requires. These classifications afford norms and ideals to emerge or to be cemented. So, it is not just about cures but notions of the norms of health. New ideals emerge that the gaze produces and then subjects people to. One outcome of this, Foucault adds, is that characteristics are then 'divided up according to the principles of the normal and the pathological' (Foucault, 2003: 41).

Fittingly, continuing this clinical theme, the data engineer is involved in what is described as a kind of interrogative practice: the diagnostic eye performs interrogations of and through the data. As this passage illustrates:

> Data integration, the practice behind integrating businesses and systems through the exchange of data, is as important and as challenging as its ever been. As Software as a Service (SaaS) becomes the new standard way for companies to operate, the need to synchronize referential data across these systems becomes increasingly critical. Not only SaaS needs up-to-date data to function, we often want to bring the data generated on their side into our data warehouse so that it can be analyzed along with the rest of our data. Sure SaaS often have their own analytics offering, but are systematically lacking the perspective that the rest of your company's data offer, so more often than not it's necessary to pull some of this data back. (Beauchemin, 2017)

Where the analysts solved puzzles, the data engineer interrogates and investigates. This interrogative observation of the data is synchronous. It looks to find ways to combine different data sources and to interface systems together in the pursuit of insights. It is about joining components into systems and bringing different data together in combinations – and then watching over these systems, adapting them, improving them, managing faults in them. Seeking perspective through data combinations, the data gaze intends to find ways to make different data work together. The gaze then comes to be interwoven in the material features of the organisation in which it is being utilised, reinforcing the connections between the infrastructure and practice. The link here is between the gaze and the architecture, with:

> ... architectural projections: like any professional in any given field of expertise, the data engineer needs to have a high level understanding of most of the tools, platforms, libraries and other resources at its disposal. The properties, use-cases and subtleties behind the different flavors of databases, computation engines, stream processors, message queues, workflow orchestrators, serialization formats and other related technologies. When designing solutions, she/he should be able to make good choices as to which technologies to use and have a vision as to how to make them work together. (Beauchemin, 2017)

The data gaze, in the hands of the data engineer, has the aim of interfacing and knitting together tools and systems to enable opportunities for observation. This is both material and temporal in its form, with data engineers creating 'a daily log of valid traffic identifiers for other teams to consume in order to produce their own metrics ... in addition to operational responsibilities [data engineers] ensure that the job finishes on time' (Irwin, 2016). The data gaze here remains foregrounded by an understanding of the infrastructure, along with the techniques and analytical grids that are required to render this functionable.

The objectivities are often to do with optimising efficiency and performance, or 'Performance tuning and optimization'.[41] The link between data and performance can be traced back to the 1970s, with notions of 'performance optimisation' and 'performance evaluation' representing a growing concern at that time (Deen, 1977). Deen's (1977: 62) account of the possibilities of databases in the 1970s pointed to the need to evaluate performance, where 'performance evaluation consists of collecting usage statistics from parameters of interest and analyzing them to find inefficient use of resources, to pinpoint bottlenecks and to identify inefficient data and storage structures'. The data gaze is directed to both the removal of inefficiency and the pursuit of value through data – in this case the value is found in honing the functioning of data systems. The data gaze, as mentioned above, is about the analytics along with the adaptability of the analytic vision. The data gaze is defined by its infrastructure. As the infrastructure changes the data gaze is intended to be responsive. Yet, in the hands of the data engineer the data gaze is also behind the formation and development of that infrastructure that then facilitates it. A complex interweaving of visions, infrastructures and practices is taking place here in this interplay between the gaze and the materialities of analytics. Changes in the scale of the infrastructure change the scale of the observation. The organisation incorporates its own clinic, of sorts, which then provides the space for the gaze to be deployed. The scale of the organisation shapes the type of codified clinic and how much of it is automated by off-the-peg or bespoke software prosthetics.

CONCLUSION

In many ways the data analyst and data engineer have come to embody the visions and promises that are attached to data. The data imaginary is embedded in the role and expectations placed upon these figures. Data analysts and data engineers are burdened with the responsibility of making those dreams real, of turning the data imaginary into something tangible. They are expected to translate, to render digestible, to find value. There are some traces of a clinical discourse in places, especially around the sanitisation and cleaning of data, but this is by no means directly comparable with the protagonists, forms of knowledge or the clinical spaces described in Foucault's *The Birth of the Clinic*. A form of expert knowledge has developed in how these data are described and how they are analysed, yet it varies somewhat from the type of fixed, demarcated and qualified gaze Foucault described.

Particularly notable in all this is the way that the expansion of data-led processes have necessitated a new set of demarcated roles. A crucial distinction emerges when exploring the division of labour in data analysis. When looking at data analysts and data engineers we discover that there are two types of diagnosis going on. There are the diagnostics that the analysts conduct directly with the data.

This is where data analysts use data to try to discover, reveal and create insights. In addition to this, there are also the diagnostics that inform, build and maintain the infrastructures in which analysis occurs. The data gaze is also behind the constant revision and debugging of these systems. The data engineer keeps an eye on the codified clinic. As such, their presence offers a sense of stability, security and accuracy to the products that then emerge from those analytic spaces. The data gaze has a diagnostic eye that takes in the data *and* the data systems. The data gaze, it would seem, watches over itself.

The two key figures here are not the only ones able to deploy a data gaze. The data gaze is not as contained to the expert figure as the clinical gaze described by Foucault, as we have already seen in Chapter 2. Despite this, these figures instead deploy a particular circumscribed and professionalised version of the data gaze and of the discourse around this gaze. This cultivated professional data gaze is rooted in both a knowledge of how to handle raw data along with a working knowledge of platforms, techniques and infrastructures. The data gaze can be deployed by other actors once those actors have the support of automated and intuitive software systems, at least that is how it is presented. Only the expert is presented as being able to handle raw data, to manage different software and to have an eye for a puzzle. The diagnostic eye described in this chapter is much more attached to expert knowledge, qualification and an accumulated knowledge of the data and systems than was suggested by the data imaginary covered earlier in this book. The result is a data gaze that is about the systems themselves as much as it is about the data. It is about problems and puzzle solving, it is about having an eye for the right types of data and an understanding of the organisational role of data in terms of identifying and finding opportunities for value. It is not just about finding patterns, it is about knowing which patterns are seen to matter. Enveloped in notions of interestingness, it is in such evaluations of patterns that analytical grids are applied.

The data engineer has an eye on the flow of data across the data infrastructures, the analyst seeks to find patterns and solve puzzles. These figures work in collaboration – with the gaze of the engineer facilitating the gaze of the analyst. The data gaze may be transferred to other actors, but it is here, in the hands of these two key figures, that it is seen to be most refined. Also, these actors, often, make it possible for others to work with data or to find narratives in those data. So, we see the data gaze is rooted in a form of qualified expertise whilst other forms of the data gaze, with less authenticity and legitimacy attached to them, are also possible. These less expert forms of the gaze get their authority from the automated systems upon which they rely. We can differentiate here by thinking of the qualified expert's diagnostic eye. This diagnostic eye of the expert is targeted, purposefully glancing, knowing where to look as it finds or solves particular issues, problems or questions. It may draw upon automated systems to do this, yet the expert does not wish to be seen to solely rely on such prosthetics.

Inevitably the dynamism envisioned in the infrastructure (discussed in Chapter 4) is reflected in the practices of data analysts and engineers. They are expected to keep on top of the changing infrastructure and to be actively shaping and reshaping their use of software components. The urgency of the data gaze and *the need for speed* covered in Chapter 3 move from the data imaginary and through the infrastructure to become embodied in the data analyst and data engineer. Their glance must, in this logic, be quick and must diagnose rapidly. The puzzles should not be studiously or carefully unpacked, they must be rapid, instant and a product of custom-fitted and up-to-date sets of components. The urgency of the data imaginary becomes implicitly embodied in the impulse to solve puzzles, in the drive to build ever quicker and more automated systems, and in the call to spot problems or faults.

Despite the broadening of data analysis across different sectors and organisations, these expert figures remain important. It is crucial to see how there are different versions of the data gaze in operation, and to explore the different levels of authority that they hold. It is also important to see how expertise is marked out where anyone can use software to turn themselves into a data analyst. As an opening and starting point for exploration, this chapter has shown how the data imaginary does not just become embedded in the data infrastructure it also becomes embodied in the data worker. There is much more to be done to understand these figures and the powerful practices in which they engage.

NOTES

1. 'A day in the life of a data analyst' – includes a series of interviews with data analysts talking about their practices, https://vimeo.com/195048661 (accessed 4 April 2017).
2. 'An interview with a real data engineer' on the Master's in Data Science site, http://www.mastersindatascience.org/careers/data-engineer/ (accessed 6 November 2017).
3. 'A day in the life of a data analyst', https://vimeo.com/195048661 (accessed 4 April 2017).
4. Ibid.
5. This definition is taken from the analytics community guide M Mode and is available at https://community.modeanalytics.com/sql/tutorial/data-wrangling-with-sql/ (accessed 7 September 2017).
6. This is taken from SeatleDataGuy's 'Intro to data analysis for everyone! Part 2', *Towards Data Science*, 18 September 2017, https://medium.com/towards-data-science/data-analysis-for-everyone-part-2-cf1c79441940 (accessed 6 November 2017).
7. This is taken from SeatleDataGuy's 'Intro to data analysis for everyone! Part 1', *Towards Data Science*, 18 September 2017, https://medium.com/towards-data-science/intro-to-data-analysis-for-everyone-part-1-ff252c3a38b5 (accessed 6 November 2017).

8. 'An interview with a data analyst', https://www.youtube.com/watch?v=kNn FA5hxI2Q (accessed 27 February 2017).

9. Ibid.

10. 'How to be a great data analyst', https://www.youtube.com/watch?v=93x9YDJ3LZg (accessed 28 February 2017).

11. This site can be found at https://stackoverflow.com

12. 'How to be a great data analyst', https://www.youtube.com/watch?v=93x9YDJ3LZg (accessed 28 February 2017).

13. 'What it takes to be a great data analyst', https://www.youtube.com/watch?v=NSflH8wW8Ak (accessed 28 February 2017).

14. Ibid.

15. Ibid.

16. 'What does a data analyst actually do?', https://youtube/eTN5dGanB5U (accessed 4 April 2017).

17. Ibid.

18. This is taken from SeatleDataGuy's 'Intro to data analysis for everyone! Part 3', *Towards Data Science*, 18 September 2017, https://medium.com/towards-data-science/intro-to-data-analysis-for-everyone-part-3-d8f02690fba0 (accessed 6 November 2017).

19. Ibid.

20. 'What does a data analyst actually do?', https://youtube/eTN5dGanB5U (accessed 4 April 2017).

21. Ibid.

22. Ibid.

23. Ibid.

24. Ibid.

25. 'An interview with a data analyst', https://www.youtube.com/watch?v=kNn FA5hxI2Q (accessed 27 February 2017).

26. 'What it takes to be a great data analyst', https://www.youtube.com/watch?v=NSflH8wW8Ak (accessed 28 February 2017).

27. 'A day in the life of a data analyst', https://vimeo.com/195048661 (accessed 4 April 2017).

28. Ibid.

29. Ibid.

30. Ibid.

31. 'How to be a great data analyst', https://www.youtube.com/watch?v=93x9 YDJ3LZg (accessed 28 February 2017).

32. This is taken from SeatleDataGuy's 'Intro to data analysis for everyone! Part 1', *Towards Data Science*, 18 September 2017, https://medium.com/towards-data-science/intro-to-data-analysis-for-everyone-part-1-ff252c3a38b5 (accessed 6 November 2017).

33. See also the data engineer David Bianco's response to the question on the difference between data engineers and data scientists in the interview conducted for the Master's in Data Science site, which also happens to include a list of valuable

personality traits in data engineers, http://www.mastersindatascience.org/careers/data-engineer/ (accessed 6 November 2017).

34. For more on this type of 'domain expertise', see 'Data analysts vs data scientist, their roles and qualification', https://www.youtube.com/watch?v=GiWqKE-yznE (accessed 4 April 2017).

35. One such infographic can be found at Analytics Vidhya 'Job comparison – Data scientist vs data engineer vs statistician', *Analytics Vidhya*, 19 October 2015, https://www.analyticsvidhya.com/blog/2015/10/job-comparison-data-scientist-data-engineer-statistician/ (accessed 7 March 2017).

36. This is further illustrated by this description from Bemby (2017): 'broadly speaking their job is to manage the data and make sure it can be channeled as required. In some companies, this means data engineers build the underlying system that allows data scientists to efficiently do their job, e.g. at Netflix data engineers may build and maintain the infrastructure that allows data scientists to experiment with recommendation algorithms, and in other companies, the data engineering is the whole shebang, e.g. at Twitter, the biggest challenge is how to make data flow as quickly and efficiently as possible.'

37. For more on the role of data engineers, especially with regard to building and their distinct roles see also the 'Big data engineer profile' provided by Datafloq, https://datafloq.com/read/job-description-big-data-engineer/202 (accessed 6 November 2017).

38. For further evidence of this, see the list of 'Date engineer responsibilities', which is part of the descriptions of 'The life of a data engineer' outlined by Master's in Data Science, http://www.mastersindatascience.org/careers/data-engineer/ (accessed 6 November 2017).

39. It is also suggested that employers have one eye on future trends when they employ data analysts, such as in PWC's guide to the data analytics job market (see point 6 in particular), https://www.pwc.com/us/en/publications/data-science and-analytics.html (accessed 6 November 2017).

40. Further examples of the points made concerning the way organisational size and objectives lead to variable roles of data engineers and variations in the desired infrastructures can be found in guides such as AltexSoft's 'How to structure a data science team', https://www.altexsoft.com/blog/datascience/how-to-structure-data-science-team-key-models-and-roles/ (accessed 12 September 2017) and data36's 'The structure of your data team: The flow of the data in your organization' https://data36.com/data-team-structure-data-organization/ (accessed 12 September 2017).

41. 'A day in the life of a data analyst', https://vimeo.com/195048661 (accessed 4 April 2017).

Conclusion

This book has explored how a faith in data emerges and then becomes embedded or cemented in social structures and practices. These are unfolding relations. Anywhere that you find talk of data you will find powerful promises and potentials projected onto those data. This tells us something of the agenda behind the data gaze: it seeks expansion. Part of how we see with and through data is how we perceive them in the first place. The data imaginary, as I have described here, opens the door for the data gaze – it also feeds back into what the data gaze is said to be able to do. The previous chapters show how these unfolding developments create particular questions for knowledge, expertise and understanding. In particular, and a key observation on the data gaze, is that it is a gaze that watches over itself. A gaze with its own oversight coded into its infrastructures and practices. In this sense it is hyper-surveillant. It is a form of knowledge that detests absences and it will always look to fill in the gaps. It watches over itself to see how such gaps can be filled by pushing back the boundaries, expanding its apparatus and by extending its practices. Never quite satisfied with its scope and depth of vision, the imperative is to oversee and to see through. Not even the data gaze – including its infrastructure and protagonists – can escape its own scrutiny. This is tied up with the pursuit of the perfect insight and the ever more granular datafied society. By watching over itself, the data gaze expands its reach, increases the data accumulated and further embeds data-led thinking into decision making, knowledge and into ideals of the way the world should run. The data gaze does not just behold the data, it watches over its own structures and practices, always seeking to expand, to see further to leave nothing untouched. It seeks to make everything analysable and surveys its own ability to leave nothing outside its view. We see this *watching-over* in the way that the infrastructures of the codified clinic expand and mutate and we also see it embodied in the role of the data engineer. The data gaze is not only inescapable, it seeks to be ever more granular, to have ever greater scope and to be ever more central to decision making.

Foucault (2003: 140) claimed that new forms of knowledge associated with clinical analysis, bring a '*measured language* that has the measure of both the things that it described and the language in which it described them' (italics in original). This type of measured language informs and is informed by the gaze. The aim is to try to capture everything that is necessary in order to read the signs (see Veyne, 2010: 26). The aim, and this is crucial in understanding Foucault's perspective on the role of the gaze in the manifestation of truth, is what he calls 'total description' – or the 'ideal of an exhaustive description' (Foucault, 2003: 139; Gutting, 1989: 125). This is not description of the totality of the body but of the details needed to prescribe. It is based upon the idea that 'the visible and the expressible are entirely convertible' (Gutting, 1989: 126). As Foucault (2003: 142) later puts it, 'total *description* is a present and ever-withdrawing horizon' (italics in original). Total description is not a completed project, it is an ongoing aim. The pursuit of total description is something we will see driving the ongoing pursuit of greater analytical reach of the infrastructures of data analysis – where the ongoing pursuit of a perfect description is also an unending objective (see Chapter 4). This total description is concerned with creating norms against which comparisons might be made and anomalies identified. It is not total in terms of being complete description, rather it is total in terms of its atomistic depth of detail – always seeking a better reading of the signs. It is also total description in its pursuit of ever greater coverage.

The pursuit of ever greater or total description is one of the ideas that anchored the clinical gaze described in Foucault's *The Birth of the Clinic*. The data gaze shares this ambition for total description but it does so not just by containing its focus upon targeted objects, but by also seeking *a total description of its own description*. It is restless. It seeks to illuminate value and make truth. It wants to see more and to expand its analytical scope and depth. It wants to find ways to describe everything so that nothing is left outside its reach. Its very authenticity and envisioned potential are tied into this kind of vision of unbounded observation and an unconstrained ability to capture and describe. It is this very restlessness, the impulse to pursue total description, that is central to the way that the knowledge with which it is related is legitimised. The data gaze may not achieve its aims but it still has consequences. It may not match with the promises that are tied into the data imaginary, but its impact will still be tangible and substantial. Material outcomes occur when weaving the dreams of the data imaginary with the practices and structures of the data gaze. The politics of this impact is crucial to explore, especially where it pushes, judges, stresses, and so on.

The data gaze, as we have seen, is directly concerned with creating possibilities for intervention. It is not passive, in this sense. It seeks to see inside in order to shape decisions, actions and practices. It is aimed at establishing norms and values against which people and things can be judged. These norms and values emerge from the forms of knowledge explored in this book. This book is about the conditions and the carving of possibilities for interventions to be made in organisations and individual lives. From the creation of the data imaginary to the way that it is then pursued, this book is about the conditions of possibility for intervention. It outlines the conditions for a culture of intervention to find its feet (which has been elaborated in a recent exploration of workplace metrics and the pursuit of 'agility' by Moore, 2018). Data and the data gaze make these interventions possible and lend them legitimacy. In these data-led interventions, the pressures of improvement and progress that we saw in the codified clinic and in the practices of the analyst and engineer are transferred to those under the spotlight of the data gaze. The data gaze exercises pressure on those being observed and becomes a pressure in our own lives to live up to the norms, expectations and searing surveillance that the data gaze brings. As the data gaze spreads, facilitated by the promises attached to it, and as the social world takes on the properties of the codified clinic, more of everyday life is exposed to data-led reasoning and intervention. This is what is at stake in understanding the shifts in knowledge explored in this book – and it is here that an understanding of the data gaze can be used to illuminate such processes.

The data gaze may diverge from the type of clinical gaze that Foucault described, but it does share some notable properties. For instance, both seek to capture component features and turn their object of study into bits – whether that be individuals, groups, institutions or even the social world. The data gaze breaks things into data and analytic outcomes – dashboards do the work of dissecting and then reimagining the data. As a result, the data gaze sees the world in bits or as component features and characteristics. It may seek a view of the whole, but it is a whole in which components are viewed in isolation or in networks of relations that are selected to see the bits in connection – the whole is retro-fitted from the parts. It is also, like Foucault's account of the clinical gaze, a gaze that compares the fragments, and then understands the whole through those fragments. These forms of gaze share an interest in individual qualities and how they can be differentiated in ever more detail, allowing comparisons and norms to cohere. Individual properties not individual people remain the focus for the data gaze. To do this, the data gaze, like the clinical gaze, is said to produce knowledge by looking beyond the surface. It deals in three dimensions, plunging below the surface to find hidden secrets and 'truths'. From the promises to the organisation of systems and practices, the notion of using data to explore the hidden depths is maintained. Within these depths the data gaze is also seeking out abnormalities and diagnoses, yet the central motivation of the data gaze is not the cure, it is instead the pursuit of efficiency and the location of value. Similarly, when exploring the analytic spaces of the data gaze and the activities of the actors in those spaces, the authority of this knowledge was comparable with the clinical gaze in the necessity for a sanitary analytical space. The data gaze, like the clinical gaze, requires a dedicated analytical space in which the integrity of the analysis is not compromised – it is the materiality of the analytic space that varies substantially. The data gaze undoubtedly shares some features with the clinical gaze, but, as I have identified, there are some important differences.

Not least of these differences is its much greater sense of urgency. The data gaze does not patiently look upon its object, it seeks an ever speedier set of outputs and analytics – it seeks perfection in its immediacy, to the point that it promises, as part of the data imaginary, to give us the world in real-time and even to give us the future.

The book set out to explore the data gaze in relation to the visions, infrastructures and practices of data analytics. Its objective was to think about how these related to one another. As well as understanding each in isolation, a key question the book posed is how the data imaginary folds into data infrastructures and practices. It asked how these visions weave into infrastructures and practices. In short, it was interested in how these visions, infrastructures and practices related to one another within the field of data analytics. This was intended to provide the basis for exploring how the data gaze is knitted with a kind of data imaginary – which is then projected onto its systems and processes and embodied in the expectations placed on the actors. Behind all this hovers the question of how knowledge is produced and legitimated through data and data analytics. Each chapter explored the formation of that knowledge and elaborated upon the ways the data gaze was bound up with the legitimation and authentication of data-led forms of knowing.

The data imaginary is important in understanding how data frontiers are pushed back and how data-led processes intensify. Chapter 2 outlined the key features and key promises that were to be found in the data imaginary as the analytics industry projected promises and possibilities onto the data. In Chapter 3 one of those key features, speed, was elaborated to give the data gaze a mobile and temporal dimension. Chapter 3 also explored how a sense of urgency is used to promote data analytics. That chapter looked at how these analytics are founded in the idea that they enable individuals and organisations to keep up with a seemingly accelerating social world. The chapters that followed focused on how these visions find their way into the material infrastructures and activities of data analytics. The data imaginary then became the foundation for exploring how such visions permeate infrastructures and practices. Chapter 4 focused on the platforms and infrastructures of data analytics, examining how various software components provide a codified analytic space for the gaze to operate within. This chapter also discussed how the notion of an expanding and ever adapting 'ecosystem' was part of the way that it was demarcated as a space for knowledge production. The notion of continual evolution, progress and refinement are etched into these infrastructures and their understandings. Chapter 5 illustrated how the data gaze is deployed to both enable flows of data whilst also analysing the data themselves. The data gaze watches over itself, it has a double focus that takes in the infrastructures *and* the data. There was also a shift in this chapter towards an understanding of expertise. Whereas in the data imaginary from Chapter 2 it was suggested that anyone could be a data analyst and anyone could be supported by software packages to enable their data gaze, Chapter 5 showed how there was still a demarcation of expertise that was based around an in-depth understanding of the infrastructural components of the analytical space and how these components should be combined and interfaced to suit the context.

This notion of expertise is crucial to understanding the data gaze. Chapter 5 explored the professional analyst's diagnostic gaze. The division of labour of the data analytics industry showed how this expertise was demarcated. Different versions of the data gaze were then mobilised within these spaces. The focus on the expert's diagnostic eye further explored how this gaze was exercised on infrastructural conditions and data flows as well as upon analysing the data themselves. The data gaze is self-monitoring and therefore self-legitimising. Indeed, its authority is based in the idea that it is hyper-reflective and self-aware. A key ingredient is that the data gaze is said to be able to see itself and ensure its own validity.

Taken together, these chapters elaborate a vision of the data gaze in the context of the data analytics industry. The data gaze is about how we see and are seen by data, but the focus of this book is predominantly on the former. I argued from the outset that in the context of a data-rich society, there was a need to understand the intermediaries who either speak with the data or provide the means by which others can speak with those data. As a result, the possibilities of the data gaze cannot be fully elaborated in a single book. Whatever form it may take, the data gaze can only be elaborated through an understanding of how data are envisioned along with explorations of how these visions weave into the infrastructures and practices of data analytics. In other words, we can only understand the data gaze through a focus upon the relations between visions, infrastructures and practices. The argument underpinning this is that we can only understand how data are transformed into forms of knowledge if we explore the data gaze in this way. It is through the concept of the data gaze that we can open up the formation of data-founded knowledge production. As such, the data gaze provides a way into understanding how data find their way into our lives and, crucially, how they stay there, growing in reach, dynamism and influence. It takes a powerful data imaginary for the horizons of the data gaze to expand. It then takes careful collaborative work for the infrastructures that are interwoven with that data imaginary to take hold and to establish themselves in the foundations of social ordering – as was illustrated by the way that the Hadoop project found its way into so many of the key media platforms through which everyday life is conducted. Finally, the notion of expertise around data can only be understood in relation to that data imaginary and that infrastructure – this is where it draws its muscle and authenticity. As these chapters have begun to reveal, visions of the data imaginary are tightly woven into both data infrastructures and practices.

This book has explored the central concept of the data gaze, but it does so without wishing to tie this concept down within too tight a set of confines. The reason for this is that it aims to capture something of the way that data are transferred to knowledge whilst acknowledging that its style and application will inevitably vary. The chapters have shown that the data gaze is context specific and relational, despite sharing properties it is tied to the organisational context and the associated expectations, possibilities and structures. The data gaze is not a peripheral form of expertise, it is something that is now central to the operation and ordering of the social world. There is now little doubt just how central data have become to the functioning of the social world. There are lots of accounts of this, with the literature showing how data are implicit within all sort of social processes (as briefly discussed in Chapter 1). This is unlikely to change soon. We may find a growing scepticism about what data can do or what they might achieve – claims and counter-claims about the power of data circulate widely. This is in part a consequence of how compelling the data imaginary has become. The power of data analytics is not just in what they actually achieve, it is in how they are imagined. It is in how powerful these data and data analytics appear that we can find the reason for their growing presence and influence. They are presented, as we saw in Chapters 2 and 3, as the only road towards efficiency, resilience and competitiveness – where we can help ourselves, be better, hone our skills, be more informed and the like. The logic is hard to resist, especially in a context of 'platform capitalism' (Langley and Leyshon, 2017; Srnicek, 2017; and as discussed in Chapter 1). I hope this book has given some sense that these data analytics are not just technical in their scope but are rooted in a particular rationality and mode of thinking. This is a rationality in which the value to transform things, it is said, resides in the data. The answers are just waiting to be found. This opens the door for analytic approaches that can find those answers and expose hidden value. Data are said to fix bugs, remove abnormalities, drive change, render competitive, free up time, reveal what is hidden, and so on. This rationality is deeply engrained in what I have described here as the data imaginary.

As knowledge is central to the gaze, clearly expertise is a central issue. The data gaze can be used widely as the analysis becomes more mobile and as the unanchored spaces of analysis proliferate. The clinical gaze required a close proximity between the observer and the observed, the data gaze is almost always exercised at a distance, it is mediated and detached. As Chapter 2 made clear, the data imaginary is premised upon the idea that software-based analytics bypass expertise and enable anyone to develop and deploy their data gaze. However, Chapter 5 illustrated that this does not mean that expertise is no longer relevant or that the data gaze does not require qualification or knowledge-based terminology. Instead, different forms of expertise play out in the data gaze. We have experts exercising embodied and established versions of the data gaze along with novices using intuitive dashboard-based systems. This would suggest that unlike Foucault's accounts of the rise of the clinical gaze, we need to find a way to differentiate types of data gaze and the limits of their authority. This largely comes down to the knowledge and expertise of the beholder. One simple distinction here is to separate out *the automated data gaze*, which is a version of the data gaze that is not based upon expertise but on the services and functions of automated analytic software packages, from the qualified data gaze of the expert data engineer, data analyst, business analyst, data scientist, and so on (whichever label is in place). In some cases this qualified data gaze also relies upon automation, and may even be involved in designing or honing the automation of systems for others to use, but it is rooted in an understanding of those automated systems and how they operate, how they can be tweaked and adapted and also which of the many options are best for a particular task. In short, then, the knowledge of the platforms and infrastructures described in Chapter 4 becomes the means by which the data gaze is then differentiated as either being qualified or unqualified. Despite appearances to the contrary, the data gaze can be differentiated along the lines of expertise.

In demarcating expertise there is an expert terminology or rationalised objective distancing that goes on in the presentation of data analytics. The emergence of data analytics relates closely with the emergence of a way of speaking about data and what they can be used to achieve. The accounts are rich in biological metaphors of ecosystems, evolution and ecologies. These biological and environmental metaphors often fuse with ideas of data being liquid and systems being plumbed pipelines. The nature of expert knowledge and expertise varies somewhat between Foucault's clinical gaze and the data gaze described in this book, yet the role of discourse in defining expertise remains. With the idea that everyone potentially becomes their own data analyst, expertise is defended through the articulation of knowledge about data, data processes and data infrastructures. The expert is demarcated by their understanding of the data imaginary and their ability to martial the infrastructure and apparently rawer forms of data in response to that imaginary. The active automated software infrastructures and intuitive modes of analysis provided by various devices and platforms are intended to provide opportunities to spread the data gaze rather than cement it as solely the property of the expert. This does not dilute expertise, instead it provokes attempts to defend and delineate expert knowledge on one hand whilst circumscribing types of data gaze on the other. There emerges a hierarchy. When the gaze is shared in this way, through the prosthetics of automated systems, there remains an expert gaze that needs a sense of its own status. It is the terminology of data analytics along with the materialities of the infrastructure that enables this hierarchy to be maintained. The data gaze may be available to anyone but this does not mean that it eradicates expertise or the qualified expert, it just means that a hierarchy forms that affords distinction.

This points us towards a further issue of note, which relates to the mobility of the space and infrastructures that facilitate the data gaze. The analytic infrastructures mean that the clinical space is codified and can be applied anywhere. These codified clinics carry 'dreams of transcendence' (Graham, 2004b). Once the gaze is no longer bound to a dedicated space, its temporality and spatiality change. In the attempts to push back the data frontiers covered in Chapters 2 and 3, a crucial part of the data imaginary is located in the apparent immateriality of those infrastructures. Chapter 3 gave an account of what this apparent immateriality means for notions of speed-up or acceleration. The analytics are perceived to accelerate once they are unanchored. Chapter 4 explored how this type of mobile accessibility of the analytics is central to how they are coded and understood. Unlike Foucault's findings concerning the necessity of the fixed, dedicated and designed spaces of the clinic for successfully affording the expert's gaze, here the clinic has become codified, amorphous and unfixed.

One point I would like to emphasise before closing is that a more dispersed infrastructure is connected to a more dispersed gaze. The clinic, for Foucault, facilitated and contained the medical gaze. The controlled conditions lent the gaze authority and were seen to be crucial to its accuracy. The data gaze is more dispersed, both in terms of who has the authority to use it and where it is used. The clinical gaze was something that occurred *in-there*, whereas the data gaze is something that occurs *out-here*. Data analytics are far more widespread than the limited medical gaze outlined by Foucault. The different properties of the infra-structures and the authority they impart is what facilitates this difference. This dispersed infrastructure may lead to a more dispersed gaze, but it is also the infrastructure that is central to how the different types of gaze are differentiated. A more dispersed gaze does not equate to the same type of gaze being deployed by everyone. So, although these infrastructures enable the data gaze to be more dispersed spatially and in terms of those who deploy it, it is the complexity of those infrastructures that also separates out the type of gaze. The complexity of these analytic systems means that they are readily predisposed to separating out *those who use them from those who know them*.

It may not be possible to fully appreciate how the data imaginary plays out in data infrastructures and practices, they are just too tightly woven and interlaced. Despite this difficulty, these infrastructures and practices of the data gaze should not be treated as distinct from the data imaginary. My argument here is that the deployment of the gaze, including how it spreads and establishes itself, needs to be understood in terms of these relations. More than anything else, thinking of the data gaze pushes us to think about the formations of knowledge associated with data and data analytics. The data gaze is a concept that calls for us to think about how this knowledge is created, legitimated and used. It is a concept that draws attention to how authority is given to data, how expertise is demarcated and how trust is built. By drawing our focus to the intermediary systems, dis-course and actors, the data gaze can be used to reveal how power is invested in data as well as how data are then analysed to realise and maintain power struc-tures. We *see data* and are *seen by data* with greater frequency – it is by understanding how data, knowledge and legitimacy interplay with each other that we can explore what this will mean. I hope this book illustrates how an understanding of the interweaving of visions of data analytics, the data infra-structure and data practices might help us to explore the powerful presence of data in ordering and shaping our lives. The expansionist tendencies of the data gaze mean that very little of social life now exists outside the limits of what Foucault (2003: 141) once called 'a speaking eye'.

Appendix:
The Sample of Data
Analytics Companies Used
in Chapters 2 and 3

The following table details the sample created for Chapters 2 and 3. The sample was created by first searching on Google for three different combinations of terms (the Google search was used as it was imagined that this is likely to be where organisations start when they are looking for analytics expertise). These search terms were: (1) data analytics companies; (2) data analytics organisations; (3) data analytics solutions. These were felt to be the most appropriate terms that were likely to be used by organisations who were looking to try to locate data analytics services. The sample was then created using search terms 1 and 3, which created the most useful and extensive lists of the type of organisations that were being sought. Two different approaches were then used to create a list of organisations that varied in type. The top 10 for search term 1 included two recent magazine articles that provided overviews of a range of data analytics companies. *Network World* and *Forbes* magazine had both published articles on big data companies 'to watch'. These lists were used to create a list of data analytics companies that were in some way notable in the industry. I used these two magazine lists, visiting the websites of the named analytics companies, and included within my sample any companies that described themselves as providing data analytics. It was felt that some supplementary examples beyond those contained in the magazine articles were needed. I used search term 3 to locate a further six data analytics providers. To do this, I simply selected the first six companies that were listed in my Google search that in some way identified themselves as providing data analytics (excluding those that had already been included in my sample as a result of being named in one of the magazine lists). This created a sample of 34 data analytics organisations of different types, ranging from consultancy to software package providers The material was gathered between the 25th of November and the 2nd of December 2015.

Reference Number	Organisation name	Organisation URL
1	Arcadia Data	http://www.arcadiadata.com
2	Cazena	https://www.cazena.com
3	DataHero	https://datahero.com
4	DataTorrent	https://www.datatorrent.com
5	Enigma	http://enigma.io
6	Experfy	https://www.experfy.com/
7	Interana	http://www.interana.com
8	Neokami	https://www.neokami.com/
9	Mapr	https://www.mapr.com
10	Wise.io	http://www.wise.io
11	Paxata	http://www.paxata.com
12	Informatica	https://www.informatica.com
13	Syntasa	http://syntasa.com
14	Actian	http://www.actian.com
15	Tableau	http://www.tableau.com
16	Sight Machine	http://www.sightmachine.com
17	Clear Story Data	http://www.clearstorydata.com
18	Ayasdi	http://www.ayasdi.com
19	Wibi	http://www.wibidata.com
20	Tamr	http://www.tamr.com
21	Trifacta	https://www.trifacta.com
22	Cloudera	http://www.cloudera.com
23	Datameer	http://www.datameer.com
24	Premise	http://www.premise.com
25	Palantir	http://www.palantir.com
26	Teradata	http://www.teradata.co.uk
27	Splunk	http://www.splunk.com
28	Platfora	http://www.platfora.com
29	Avalon	http://www.avalonconsult.com
30	Das	http://www.dasconsultants.com
31	CSC	http://www.csc.com/big_data
32	Avanade	http://www.avanade.com
33	Oracle	https://www.oracle.com/solutions/business-analytics/index.html
34	SAP	http://go.sap.com/uk/solution/analytics.html

References

Aghabozorgi, S. and Lin, P. (2016) 'Data scientist vs data engineer', *Big Data University*, 6 June 2016, https://bigdatauniversity.com/blog/data-scientist-vs-data-engineer/ (accessed 2 March 2017).

Allen-Robertson, J. (2017) 'Critically assessing digital documents: Materiality and the interpretive role of software', *Information, Communication & Society*, online first, DOI: http://dx.doi.org/10.1080/1369118X.2017.1351575

Amoore, L. (2011) 'Data derivatives: On the emergence of a security risk calculus for our times', *Theory, Culture & Society* 28(6): 24–43.

Amoore, L. (2013) *The Politics of Possibility: Risk and Security Beyond Possibility*. Durham, NC: Duke University Press.

Amoore, L. and Hall, A. (2009) 'Taking people apart: Digitized dissection and the body at the border', *Environment and Planning D: Society and Space* 27(3): 444–64.

Andrejevic, M. (2013) *Infoglut: How Too Much Information is Changing the Way We Think and Know*. Abingdon: Routledge.

Andrejevic, M., Hearn, A. and Kennedy, H. (2015) 'Cultural studies of data mining: Introduction', *European Journal of Cultural Studies* 18(4–5): 379–94.

Ang, I. (1985) *Watching Dallas*. London: Routledge.

Armitage, J. (2001) *Virilio Live: Selected Interviews*. London: Sage.

Aschoff, N. (2015) *The New Prophets of Capital*. London: Verso.

Banerjee, S. (2014) '10 reasons why Hadoop is not the best big data platform all the time', *BPO Times*, 11 November 2014, http://www.bpotimes.com/efytimes/fullnewsbpo.asp?edid=152456 (accessed 17 July 2017).

Bartkowski, F. (1988) 'Epistemic drift in Foucault', in Diamond, I. and Quinby, L. (eds) *Feminism and Foucault: Reflections on Resistance*. Boston: Northeastern University Press. pp. 43–58.

Beauchemin, M. (2017) 'The rise of the data engineer', *freeCodeCamp*, 20 January 2017, https://medium.freecodecamp.com/the-rise-of-the-data-engineer-91be18f1e603#.at 4o5pc1n (accessed 20 February 2017).

Becker, H. (2007) *Telling about Society*. Chicago: University of Chicago Press.

Beer, D. (2013) *Popular Culture and New Media: The Politics of Circulation*. Basingstoke: Palgrave Macmillan.

Beer, D. (2016a) 'How should we do the history of big data?', *Big Data & Society* 3(1): 1–10.

Beer, D. (2016b) *Metric Power*. London: Palgrave Macmillan.

Bemby, S. (2017) 'What is data engineering?', *Hackernoon*, 5 January 2017, https://hackernoon.com/what-is-data-engineering-5334cec027d0 (accessed 12 September 2017).

Bonaci, M. (2015) 'The history of Hadoop', *Medium*, 11 April 2015, https://medium.com/@markobonaci/the-history-of-hadoop-68984a11704 (accessed 13 April 2016).

Bottici, C. (ed.) (2012) *The Politics of Imagination*. London: Routledge.

boyd, d. and Crawford, K. (2012) 'Critical questions for big data: Provocations for a cultural, technological, and scholarly phenomenon', *Information, Communication & Society* 15(5): 662–79.

Braidotti, R. (2013) *The Posthuman*. Cambridge: Polity.

Brown, N. and Michael, M. (2003) 'A sociology of expectations: *Retrospecting prospects and prospecting retrospects*', Technology Analysis & Strategic Management 15(1): 3–18.

Brown, W. (2015) *Undoing the Demos: Neoliberalism's Stealth Revolution*. New York: Zone Books.

Brust, A. (2016) 'Microsoft, MapR announce new Apache Spark-based releases', *ZDNet*, 6 June 2016, http://www.zdnet.com/article/microsoft-mapr-announce-new-apache-spark-based-releases/ (accessed 14 June 2016).

Bucher, T. (2017) 'The algorithmic imaginary: Exploring the ordinary affects of Facebook algorithms', *Information, Communication & Society* 20(1): 30–44.

Carson, C. (2016) 'The phases of Hadoop maturity: Where exactly is it going?', *DataInformed*, 16 February 2016, http://data-informed.com/phases-of-hadoop-maturity-where-exactly-is-it-going/ (accessed 2 June 2016).

Columbus, L. (2015) 'Roundup of analytics, Big data & business intelligence forecasts and market estimates, 2015', *Forbes*, 25 May 2015, http://www.forbes.com/sites/louiscolumbus/2015/05/25/roundup-of-analytics-big-data-business-intelligence-forecasts-and-market-estimates-2015/#327d14254869 (accessed 17 July 2016).

Davies, W. (2014) *The Limits of Neoliberalism: Authority, Sovereignty and the Logic of Competition*. London: Sage.

Davies, W. (2017a) 'How are we now? Real-time mood monitoring as valuation', *Journal of Cultural Economy* 10(1): 34–48.

Davies, W. (2017b) 'How statistics lost their power and why we should fear what comes next', The *Guardian*, 19 January 2017, https://www.theguardian.com/politics/2017/jan/19/crisis-of-statistics-big-data-democracy (accessed 16 October 2017).

Dean, J. (2009) *Democracy and Other Neoliberal Fantasies: Communicative Capitalism and Left Politics*. Durham, NC: Duke University Press.

Deen, S.M. (1977) *Fundamentals of Data Base Systems*. London and Basingstoke: Macmillan.

Derrida, J. (1996) *Archive Fever: A Freudian Impression*. Chicago: University of Chicago Press.

Diaconita, V. (2015) 'Approaches for parallel data loading and data querying', *Database Systems Journal* 11(1): 78–85.

Dodge, M. and Kitchin, R. (2009) 'Software, objects, and home space', *Environment and Planning A* 41(6): 1344–65.

Dossman, C. (2017) 'Becoming a machine learning engineer', *Towards Data Science*, 3 November 2017, https://medium.com/towards-data-science/becoming-a-machine-learning-engineer-step-5-build-a-portfolio-31d219e40fbc (accessed 6 November 2017).

Doughty, K. and Murray, L. (2016) 'Discourses of mobility: Institutions, everyday lives and embodiment', *Mobilities* 11(2): 303–22.

Douglas, C. and Curino, C. (2015) 'Blind men and an elephant: Coalescing open-source, academic, and industrial perspectives on BigData', *IEEE 31st International Conference on Data Engineering*, 13–17 April 2015. pp. 1523–6.

Dreyfus, H.L. and Rabinow, P. (1982) *Michel Foucault: Beyond Structuralism and Hermeneutics*. New York: Harvester Wheatsheaf.

During, S. (1992) *Foucault and Literature: Towards a Genealogy of Writing*. London: Routledge.

Džeroski, S. (2001) 'Data mining in a nutshell', in Džeroski, S. and Lavrač, N. (eds) *Relational Data Mining*. London: Springer. pp. 3–27.

Džeroski, S. and Lavrač, N. (2001) 'Preface', in Džeroski, S. and Lavrač, N. (eds) *Relational Data Mining*. London: Springer. pp. vii–ix.

Eremenko, K. (2017) '45 ways to activate your data science career', *Towards Data Science*, 30 October 2017, https://medium.com/towards-data-science/45-ways-to-activate-your-data-science-career-6a0d9c664e84 (accessed 6 November 2017).

Eribon, D. (1992) *Michel Foucault*. London: Faber.

Espeland, W.N. and Sauder, M. (2007) 'Rankings and reactivity: How public measures recreate social worlds', *American Journal of Sociology 113*(1): 1–40.

Feldman, R. and Hirsh, H. (1998) 'Finding associations in collections of text', in Michalski, R.S., Bratko, I. and Kubat, M. (eds) *Machine Learning and Data Mining: Methods and Applications*. Chichester: John Wiley. pp. 223–40.

Foucault, M. (1980) *Power/Knowledge: Selected Interviews and Other Writings 1972–1979*. Ed. Gordon, C. New York: Pantheon.

Foucault, M. (1986) *Death and the Labyrinth: The World of Raymond Roussel*. Berkeley: University of California Press.

Foucault, M. (1991) *Discipline and Punish: The Birth of the Prison*. London: Penguin.

Foucault, M. (2003) *The Birth of the Clinic*. Abingdon: Routledge.

Gane, N. (2006) 'Speed up or slow down? Social theory in the information age', *Information, Communication & Society 9*(1): 20–38.

Gane, N. (2012) 'The governmentalities of neoliberalism: Panopticism, post-panopticism and beyond', *Sociological Review 60*(4): 611–34.

Gardiner, M.E. (2017) 'Critique of accelerationism', *Theory, Culture & Society 34*(1): 29–52.

Gardner, J. (2017) 'Patient-centred medicine and the broad clinical gaze: Measuring outcomes in paediatric deep brain stimulation', *Biosocieties 12*(2): 239–56.

Gitelman, L. (ed.) (2013) *'Raw Data' is an Oxymoron*. Cambridge, MA: MIT Press.

Gitelman, L. and Jackson, V. (2013) 'Introduction', in Gitelman, L. (ed.) *'Raw Data' is an Oxymoron*. Cambridge, MA: MIT Press. pp. 1–14.

Graham, S. (2004a) 'Beyond the "dazzling light": From dreams of transcendence to the "remediation" of urban life: a research manifesto', *New Media & Society 6*(1): 16–25.

Graham, S. (2004b) 'Introduction: From dreams of transcendence to the remediation of urban life', in Graham, S. (ed.) *The Cybercities Reader*. London: Routledge. pp. 1–30.

Gutting, G. (1989) *Michel Foucault's Archaeology of Scientific Reason*. Cambridge: Cambridge University Press.

Gutting, G. (1994) 'Introduction: Michel Foucault: A user's manual', in Gutting, G. (ed.) *The Cambridge Companion to Foucault*. Cambridge: Cambridge University Press. pp. 1–27.

Han, J. and Kamber, M. (2001) *Data Mining: Concepts and Techniques*. San Francisco: Morgan Kaufmann Publishers.

Han Lee, C. (2014) '3 data careers decoded and what it means for you', *Udacity*, 10 December 2014, http://blog.udacity.com/2014/12/data-analyst-vs-data-scientist-vs-data-engineer.html (accessed 7 March 2017).

Hand, D., Mannila, H. and Smyth, P. (2001) *Principles of Data Mining*. Cambridge, MA: MIT Press.

Hand, M., Shove, E. and Southerton, D. (2005) 'Explaining showering: A discussion of the material, conventional, temporal dimensions of practice', *Sociological Research Online* 10(2): http://www.socresonline.org.uk/10/2/hand.html

Haraway, D. (1991) *Simians, Cyborgs, and Women: The Reinvention of Nature*. London: Free Association Books.

Harris, D. (2013) 'The history of Hadoop: From 4 nodes to the future of data', *Gigaom*, 4 May 2013, https://gigaom.com/2013/03/04/the-history-of-hadoop-from-4-nodes-to-the-future-of-data/ (accessed 13 April 2016).

Harrison, G. (2015) *Next Generation Databases*. New York: Apress.

Hendy, A. (2015) 'Arjun Murthy discusses the future of Hadoop', *SD Times*, 19 October 2015, http://sdtimes.com/arun-murthy-discusses-the-future-of-hadoop/ (accessed 2 June 2016).

Howe, D.R. (1983) *Data Analysis for Data Base Design*. London: Edward Arnold.

Inmon, W.H. (1996) *Building the Data Warehouse*. 2nd edn. New York: John Wiley.

Insight Fellows Program (2014) 'Data science vs data engineering', *Insight*, 7 August 2014, https://blog.insightdatascience.com/data-science-vs-data-engineering-62da7 678adaa#.9f1q215s9 (accessed 1 March 2017).

Irwin, R. (2016) 'A day in the life of a data engineer', *Insight*, 28 October 2016, https://blog.insightdatascience.com/a-day-in-the-life-of-a-data-engineer-35efacaa6b2e#.l1ue6okvd (accessed 1 March 2017).

Jay, M. (1986) 'In the empire of the gaze: Foucault and the denigration of vision in twentieth-century French thought', in Hoy, D.C. (ed.) *Foucault: A Critical Reader*. Oxford: Blackwell. pp. 175–99.

Jha, S., Qiu, J., Luckow, A., Mantha, P. and Fox, G.C. (2014) 'A tale of two data-intensive paradigms: Applications, abstractions, and architectures', *2014 IEEE International Congress on Big Data*, 27 June–2 July 2014, https://doi.org/10.1109/BigData.Congress.2014.137 (accessed 14 June 2016).

Kamal, K.C. and Anyanwu, K. (2010) 'Scheduling Hadoop jobs to meet deadlines', *2010 IEEE Second International Conference on Cloud Computing Technology and Science* 30 November–3 December 2010, https://doi.org/10.1109/CloudCom.2010.97 (accessed 25 April 2016).

Karppi, T. and Crawford, K. (2016) 'Social media, financial algorithms and the hack crash', *Theory, Culture & Society* 33(1): 73–92.

Kearns, G. (2007) 'The history of medical geography after Foucault', in Crampton, J.W. and Elden, S. (eds) *Space, Knowledge and Power*. Farnham: Ashgate. pp. 205–222.

Kennedy, H. (2016) *Post, Mine, Repeat: Data Mining Becomes Ordinary*. London: Palgrave Macmillan.

Kennedy, H., Hill, R., Allen, W. and Aiello, G. (2016) 'The work that visualisation conventions do', *Information, Communication & Society* 19(16): 715–35.

Kennedy, H., Poell, T. and van Dijck, J. (2015) 'Data and agency', *Big Data & Society* 2(2): 1–7. DOI: 10.1177/2053951715621569

Kitchin, R. (2014) *The Data Revolution: Big Data, Open Data, Data Infrastructures and Their Consequences*. London: Sage.

Knorr Cetina, K. (1994) 'Primitive classification and postmodernity: Towards a sociological notion of fiction', *Theory, Culture & Society* 11(1): 1–22.

Kwan, A. (2015) 'The science/engineering divide', *Towards Data Science*, 13 July 2015, https://medium.com/towards-data-science/data-science-vs-data-engineering-b905077b2c2d#.lwws2ri0e (accessed 1 March 2017).

Langley, P. and Leyshon, A. (2017) 'Platform capitalism: The intermediation and capitalisation of digital economic circulation', *Finance and Society* 3(1): 11–31.

Lash, S. (2002) *Critique of Information*. London: Sage.

Lash, S. (2010) *Intensive Culture: Social Theory, Religion and Contemporary Capitalism*. London: Sage.

Lash, S. and Lury, C. (2007) *The Global Culture Industry: The Mediation of Things*. Cambridge: Polity.

Le, J. (2017) 'The 10 statistical techniques data scientists need to master', *Towards Data Science*, 31 October 2017, https://medium.com/towards-data-science/the-10-statistical-techniques-data-scientists-need-to-master-1ef6dbd531f7 (accessed 6 November 2017).

Leonelli, S., Rappert, B. and Davies, G. (2017) 'Data shadows: Knowledge, openness, and absence', *Science, Technology & Human Values* 42(2): 191–202.

Luckow, A., Kennedy, K., Manhardt, F., Djerekarov, E., Vorster, B. and Apon, A. (2015) 'Automotive big data: Applications, workloads and infrastructures', *2015 IEEE International Conference on Big Data*, 29 October–1 November 2015, https://doi.org/10.1109/BigData.2015.7363874 (accessed 14 June 2016).

Lupton, D. (2016) *The Quantified Self*. Cambridge: Polity.

Macey, D. (1995) *The Lives of Michel Foucault*. New York: Vintage.

Mackenzie, C. (2015) 'The latest trends in the Hadoop project', *The ServerSide*, August 2015, http://www.theserverside.com/podcast/The-latest-trends-in-the-Hadoop-project (accessed 12 July 2017).

Maiers, C. (2017) 'Analytics in action: Users and predictive data in the neonatal intensive care unit', *Information, Communication & Society* 20(6): 915–29.

Mannila, H. (2001) 'Foreword', in Džeroski, S. and Lavrač, N. (eds) *Relational Data Mining*. London: Springer. pp. v–vi.

McMullan, T. (2015) 'What does the panopticon mean in the age of digital surveillance?', The *Guardian*, 23 July 2015, https://www.theguardian.com/technology/2015/jul/23/panopticon-digital-surveillance-jeremy-bentham (accessed 10 August 2017).

McNay, L. (1994) *Foucault: A Critical Introduction*. Cambridge: Polity Press.

Metz, C. (2011) 'How Yahoo spawned Hadoop, the future of big data', *Wired*, 18 October 2011, https://www.wired.com/2011/10/how-yahoo-spawned-hadoop/ (accessed 13 April 2016).

Michalski, R.S., Bratko, I. and Kubat, M. (eds) (1998a) *Machine Learning and Data Mining: Methods and Applications*. Chichester: John Wiley.

Michalski, R.S., Rosenfeld, A., Duric, Z., Maloof, M. and Zhang, Q. (1998b) 'Learning patterns in images', in Michalski, R.S., Bratko, I. and Kubat, M. (eds) *Machine Learning and Data Mining: Methods and Applications*. Chichester: John Wiley. pp. 241–68.

Mitchell, W.J. (2003) *Me++: The Cyborg Self in the Networked City*. Cambridge, MA: MIT Press.

Mohammed, J. (2015) 'Is Apache Spark going to replace Hadoop?', *Aptuz*, 20 March 2015, http://aptuz.com/blog/is-apache-spark-going-to-replace-hadoop/ (accessed 2 June 2016).

Moore, P. (2018) *The Quantified Self in Precarity: Work, Technology and What Counts*. Abingdon: Routledge.

Neff, G. and Nafus, D. (2016) *Self-Tracking*. Cambridge, MA: MIT Press.

Nettleton, S. (1992) *Power, Pain and Dentistry*. Buckingham: Open University Press.

O'Farrell, C. (2005) *Michel Foucault*. London: Sage.

Oliver, A.C. (2016) '!6 for '16: What you must know about Hadoop and Spark right now', *InfoWorld*, 8 January 2016, http://www.infoworld.com/article/3019754/application-development/16-things-you-should-know-about-hadoop-and-spark-right-now.html (accessed 2 June 2016).

Olston, C., Reed, B., Srivastava, U., Kumar, R. and Tomkins, A. (2008) 'Pig Latin: A not-so-foreign language for data processing', *SIGMOD' 08*, 9–12 June 2008, Vancouver, http://infolab.stanford.edu/~olston/publications/sigmod08.pdf (accessed 18 July 2016).

Osborne, T. (1992) 'Medicine and epistemology: Michel Foucault and the liberality of clinical reason', *History of the Human Sciences* 5(2): 63–93.

Pasquale, F. (2015) *The Black Box Society: The secret algorithms that control money and information*. Cambridge, MA: Harvard University Press.

Peck, J. (2010) *Constructions of Neoliberal Reason*. Oxford: Oxford University Press.

Peck, J. and Theodore, N. (2007) 'Variegated capitalism', *Progress in Human Geography* 31(6): 731–72.

Pola, N.M. (2015) 'Decoding Pig: The data toolkit of Hadoop', *PC Quest*, 18 December 2015, http://www.pcquest.com/decoding-pig-the-data-toolkit-of-hadoop/ (accessed 2 June 2016).

Porter, T.M. (1995) *Trust in Numbers: The Pursuit of Objectivity in Science and Public Life*. Princeton, NJ: Princeton University Press.

Puschmann, C. and Burgess, J. (2014) 'Metaphors of big data', *International Journal of Communication* 8: 1690–709.

Raffnsøe, S., Gudmand-Høyer, M. and Thaning, M.S. (2016) *Michel Foucault: A Research Companion*. Basingstoke: Palgrave Macmillan.

Ramel, D. (2016) '5 most active Apache big data projects', *ADTmag*, 5 March 2016, https://adtmag.com/blogs/dev-watch/2016/05/asf-big-data-projects.aspx (accessed 12 July 2016).

Ren, K., Kwon, Y., Balazinska, M. and Howe, B. (2013) 'An analysis of Hadoop usage in scientific workloads', *Proceedings of the VLDB Endowment* 6(10): 1–12.

Rosa, H. (2003) 'Social acceleration: Ethical and political consequences of a desynchronized high-speed society', *Constellations* 10(1): 3–33.

Rosenberg, D. (2013) 'Data before the fact', in Gitelman, L. (ed.) *'Raw Data' is an Oxymoron*. Cambridge, MA: MIT Press.

Ruppert, E., Harvey, P., Lury, C., Mackenzie, A., McNally, R., Baker, S.A., Kallianos, Y. and Lewis, C. (2015) *Socialising big data: From concept to practice*. CRESC Working Paper No. 138, http://www.cresc.ac.uk/medialibrary/workingpapers/wp138.pdf

Saha, B., Shah, H., Seth, S., Vijayaraghavan, G., Murthy, A. and Curino, C. (2016) 'Apache Tez: A unifying framework for modelling and building data processing applications', *SIGMOD' 15*, 31 May–4 June 2016, Melbourne, https://www.cse.ust.hk/~weiwa/teaching/Fall16-COMP6611B/reading_list/Tez.pdf (accessed 14 June 2016).

Sanyal, K. (2007) *Rethinking Capitalist Development: Primitive Accumulation, Governmentality and Post-colonial Capitalism*. Abingdon: Routledge.

Sassatelli, R. (2011) 'Interview with Laura Mulvey: Gender, gaze and technology in film culture', *Theory, Culture & Society* 28(5): 123–43.

Sassen, S. (2006) *Territory, Authority, Rights: From Medieval to Global Assemblages*. Princeton, NJ: Princeton University Press.

Savage, M. (2013) 'The "social life of methods": A critical introduction', *Theory, Culture & Society* 30(4): 3–21.

Schmidt, K. (2015) 'Data engineer vs data scientist vs business analyst', *Towards Data Science*, 22 March 2015, https://medium.com/towards-data-science/data-engineer-vs-data-scientist-vs-business-analyst-b68d201364bc#.ewql7ocsr (accessed 1 March 2017).

Schrock, A. and Shaffer, G. (2017) 'Data ideologies of an interested public: A study of grassroots open government data intermediaries', *Big Data & Society* 4(1). DOI: 10.1177/2053951717690750

Schwan, A. and Shapiro, S. (2011) *How to Read Foucault's Discipline and Punish*. London: Pluto Press.

Sharon, T. (2017) 'Self-tracking for health and the quantified self: Re-articulating autonomy, solidarity, and authenticity in an age of personalized healthcare', *Philosophy & Technology* 30(1): 93–121.

Siisiäinen, L. (2013) *Foucault and the Politics of Hearing*. Abingdon: Routledge.

Simon, A.R. (1997) *Data Warehousing for Dummies*. Foster City, CA: IDG Books.

Singh, S., Singh, P., Garg, R. and Mishra, P.K. (2015) 'Big data: Technologies, trends and applications', *International Journal of Computer Science and Information Technologies* 6(5): 4633–9.

Srnicek, N. (2017) *Platform Capitalism*. Cambridge: Polity.

Stata, R. (2016) 'Under the hood of Hadoop: Its journey from open source to self-service', *Data Centre Knowledge*, 12 April 2016, http://www.datacenterknowledge.com/archives/2016/04/12/hood-hadoop-journey-open-source-self-service/ (accessed 13 April 2016).

Stein, J. (2016) 'Data engineers vs. data scientists', *Stitch Data*, 29 September 2016, https://blog.stitchdata.com/data-engineer-vs-data-scientist-the-difference-according-to-linkedin-e0bee6248fd4#.7fbtu3fui, (accessed 1 March 2017).

Taylor, C. (2004) *Modern Social Imaginaries*. Durham, NC: Duke University Press.

Taylor, R.C. (2010) 'An overview of the Hadoop/MapReduce/HBase framework and its current applications in bioinformatics', *BMC Bioinformatics* 11(12) (S1): 1–6.

Thrift, N. (2005) *Knowing Capitalism*. London: Sage.

Tiyyagura, N.S., Rallabandi, M. and Nalluri, R. (2016) 'Data migration from RDBMS to Hadoop', *All Capstone Projects*. Paper 184.

Tomlinson, J. (2007) *The Culture of Speed: The Coming of Immediacy*. London: Sage.

Turow, J., McGuigan, L. and Maris, E.R. (2015) 'Making data mining a part of life: Physical retailing, customer surveillance and the 21st century social imaginary', *European Journal of Cultural Studies* 18(4–5): 464–78.

Tyler, I. (2015) 'Classificatory struggles: Class, culture and inequality in neoliberal times', *The Sociological Review* 63(2): 493–511.

Urry, J. (1990) *The Tourist Gaze: Leisure and Travel in Contemporary Societies*. London: Sage.

van Dijck, J. (2014) 'Datafication, dataism and dataveillance: Big data between scientific paradigm and ideology', *Surveillance & Society* 12(2): 197–208.

Vavilapalli, V.K., Murthy, A.C., Douglas, C., Agarwal, S., Konar, M., Evans, R., Graves, T., Lowe, J., Shah, H., Seth, S., Saha, B., Curino, C., O'Malley, O., Radia, S., Reed, B. and Baldeshwieler, E. (2013) 'Apache Hadoop YARN: Yet another resource negotiator', *SoCC 2013*, 1–3 October 2013, Santa Clara, CA, http://dx.doi.org/10.1145/2523633 (accessed 14 June 2016).

Vesset, D., McDonough, B., Schubmehl, D., Olofson, C.W., Woodward, A. and Bond, S. (2015) 'Worldwide business analytics software market shares, 2014', *IDC*, http://www.sas.com/content/dam/SAS/en_us/doc/analystreport/idc-business-analytics-software-market-shares-108014.pdf (accessed 18 July 2016).

Veyne, P. (2010) *Foucault: His Thoughts, His Character*. Cambridge: Polity.

Virilio, P. (1991) *Lost Dimension*. New York: Semiotext(e).

Vostal, F. (2017) 'Slowing down modernity: A critique', *Time & Society*, online first, DOI: 10.1177/0961463X17702163

Wajcman, J. (2015) *Pressed for Time: The Acceleration of Life in Digital Capitalism*. Chicago: University of Chicago Press.

Williamson, B. (2017) 'Computing brains: Learning algorithms and neurocomputation in the smart city', *Information, Communication & Society* 20(1): 81–99.

Wodehouse, C. (2016) 'SQL vs. NoSQL databases: What's the difference?', *B2C*, 9 May 2016, http://www.business2community.com/brandviews/upwork/sql-vs-nosql-databases-whats-difference-01539315#yd4AUaflUT6tpK6t.97 (accessed 31 May 2016).

Wolpe, T. (2014) 'Hadoop's Tez: Why winning Apache's top level status matters', *ZDNet*, 23 July 2014, http://www.zdnet.com/article/hadoops-tez-why-winning-apaches-top-level-status-mtters/ (accessed 14 June 2016).

Woodie, A. (2015) 'From spiders to elephants: The history of Hadoop', *Datanami*, 15 April 2015, https://www.datanami.com/2015/04/15/from-spiders-to-elephants-the-history-of-hadoop/ (accessed 13 April 2016).

Woodie, A. (2016) 'Why Hadoop must evolve toward greater simplicity', *Datanami*, 15 March 2016, https://www.datanami.com/2016/03/15/hadoop-must-evolve-toward-greater-simplicity/ (accessed 15 March 2016).

Woolgar, S. (ed.) (2002) *Virtual Society? Technology, Cyberbole, Reality*. Oxford: Oxford University Press

Yadav, P.P., Babu, A.S. and Saritha, S.J. (2014) 'A new era of Hadoop – Hadoop 2.X', *International Journal of Scientific & Engineering Research* 5(9): 508–11.

Index